BUSINESS COMES TO THE
EXPERT

A PROACTIVE MARKETING PLAN
FOR PROFESSIONAL PRACTICE FIRMS

östberg

Library of Design Management

✚ Greenway Communications

ISBN: 9780978555252

Östberg Library of Design Management

Greenway Communications, LLC, a division of The Greenway Group

25 Technology Parkway South, Suite 101

Norcross, GA 30092

800.726.8603

www.greenway.us

First Printing

Layout Design: Dan Downey

Cover Design: Austin Cramer

BUSINESS COMES TO THE
EXPERT

A PROACTIVE MARKETING PLAN FOR PROFESSIONAL PRACTICE FIRMS

BRENDA RICHARDS
KATHLEEN SOLDATI

ACKNOWLEDGEMENTS

Two things were confirmed for me during the development and documentation of this book: Kathleen Soldati is both a dynamic marketing guru and an excellent writing partner. Thank you, Kathleen, for saying yes to the idea of writing a book and for finding the hours to diligently refine the manuscript.

Numerous associates supported me during my 25-year career in professional services, and I am grateful for their help and many kindnesses as well as their keen business sense. In regard to this book, I must individually thank my husband, David, for sacrificing his time with me; my children and my extended family for faultless support; my principals at JSA Inc., James H. Somes, FAIA, and James M. Warner, FAIA, for being great friends, for providing me opportunities and for always educating; and the glorious and famous Queens for always making me laugh.

Brenda L. Richards, SDA, Hon. AIA

To Brenda: Thank you for approaching me with the idea for this book, for nudging me, and for being with me every step of the way. I'd like to thank my husband and mainstay, Lincoln, my four children, and my friends for their support. I've had several mentors in my career—Ed Mallon, Neil Fox, Edith Grodin, Richard Fitzgerald—who were generous with their guidance. Over 35 years, I've learned so much from all my employers, employees, co-workers, partners, clients, and students. What I learned about architectural marketing from Jim Warner and Jim Somes was invaluable. Thanks to the Boston Architectural College for offering me a place to teach. I particularly would like to note the collegiality of the Boston Society of Architects and the Boston and Maine chapters, and the national organization of the Society for Marketing Professional Services. Finally, a special thanks to Dr. Chris Barlow of The Co-Creativity Institute.

Kathleen Soldati

INTRODUCTION

1

WHAT DOES "BUSINESS COMES TO THE EXPERT" MEAN?

We recently heard the following advice from a young person on how to market to young people: "We don't want you to come to us. We want you to give us a reason to find you." That comment is the essence of the adage "Business comes to the expert." Your audience needs to be aware of your knowledge and expertise, and your audience needs to perceive that knowledge and expertise as beneficial in order for them to seek you out. To build that awareness, it is essential that you share your knowledge through the vehicles your audience is paying attention to—advertising, newsletters, e-mail, columns, articles, panel discussions, or seminars.

In order to promote both your firm's and your designers' expertise, you must start by assessing the knowledge your firm possesses. You will learn to disseminate this knowledge in a way that will result in your designers being recognized as the go-to experts.

Keep two ideas in mind as you read this book. First, it is focused on *proactive* marketing rather than reactive marketing. Reactive marketing— replying to advertised needs, such as Requests for Proposals—is a necessary component to successful marketing, but this book is all about being proactive with marketing. In it, you will learn about looking at and understanding what knowledge your firm possesses, what your clients and prospects need, and creating awareness in the marketplace of your firm as the go-to experts.

Second, it is focused on how to *think* about marketing. We believe if you meet your marketing challenges armed with an overall approach, not just single strategies for building your business, it will be that much easier for you to meet any marketing challenge.

To demonstrate how best to use the concepts, strategies, and worksheets contained in *Business Comes to the Expert*, we created a fictional firm known as ABC Design. The profile of ABC Design is that it is an urban firm providing design services in three markets—two primary: senior living and healthcare, and one secondary: education—with strong skills in historic preservation and sustainability. The firm has an annual gross income of $4 million, 7% of which is dedicated to its marketing budget, including allocated salaries and all other marketing costs.

The purpose of this book is to assist you in creating your marketing plan, managing it well on a daily basis, and driving business to your firm.

GETTING STARTED

Most designers begin the marketing process by using their natural, entrepreneurial instincts. They start broadcasting the fact that they are in business by using their personal network, but eventually they recognize that they have reached the point where they need to create a formal marketing plan. This is often prompted by aspirations for more sophisticated clients, higher income, wider geographic range, or more complex projects. To reach those goals, a focused plan becomes a necessity.

In the beginning, designers use their connections in their inner circle of friends and acquaintances to build a client base and establish themselves, but once that inner circle is penetrated, increased exposure and awareness are critical. If increased exposure in your markets is a vision you have for the future of your firm, you need a plan to help you reach that goal.

To get results from the process outlined in this book, make a commitment to setting aside specific time to devote to your plan. Focus on completing research and then on accomplishing your stated goals. Because a successful marketing plan requires someone in charge, you must be willing either to be that person or to give that authority to someone who will manage your plan and report to you. Marketing is a team effort, but the best results are realized when the leader leads. Even with a well-defined and fully staffed marketing department, the Principal in Charge of Marketing must be prepared to stay on top of marketing decisions and activities, from attending annual conferences to conducting publicity campaigns.

Often, firms go through the planning process, conduct the research, and write the marketing plan only for it to end up on a shelf, never to be looked at again. What a waste! The missing piece of the scenario is managing the execution of the marketing plan.

The plan you write, based on this book, will result in a simple management tool we have all used—the To-Do List. You will develop this list of tasks, responsible parties, and deadlines, and use it as your daily task list, as the agenda for your weekly marketing meetings, and as the guiding light for all of your marketing reports, whether weekly, monthly, quarterly, or annually. And the great thing is that once you use it as your annual plan, it is the basis for your next year's plan, with modifications, of course.

We believe that the *managing* of marketing is as important as the marketing and that, without the managing, you will not achieve all you are capable of in marketing your firm. And it is our intention that your plan will not gather dust on a shelf but will, in fact, be a dog-eared, scribbled-on To-Do List that will be the first thing you look at each morning when you arrive at the office and the last thing you look at each night before you leave. That being said, here is an overview of the concepts to be discussed throughout this book.

CONCEPT: PERSONAL EXPERIENCE WITH MARKETING

It is helpful to realize that you may know more about marketing than you now imagine. For your entire life, as a consumer, you have been one half of the marketing equation. What you know as a consumer is as critical as what any professional marketer knows and that knowledge will help you achieve marketing success. You know the marketing approaches that you like and you know what you do not like. You read, watch, and listen to various media outlets, whether they are consumer, business or trade. You know how you like to be reached. Having the attitude that you already have some expertise in marketing is critical since you will be able to not only bring all of this information to bear on what you will do to successfully market your organization, but it will give you the confidence to carry out your marketing tasks.

CONCEPT: MARKETING STARTS WITH KNOWLEDGE MANAGEMENT

Although not listed on the balance sheet, knowledge is one of your firm's greatest assets. The knowledge you use to design buildings is what you use to signal to the marketplace that you possess what the prospect is looking for. Knowledge informs the messages you disseminate. It builds awareness of your firm as experts. It brings business to your door. As a result, you can see that knowledge is the foundation of marketing. In order to use that knowledge to maximum benefit, it must be managed. It needs to be catalogued and stored for easy retrieval, distilled into easily digestible pieces, and regularly disseminated via various vehicles to specific audiences. In Chapter Two, we will talk further about Knowledge Management.

CONCEPT: BOOK OF KNOWLEDGE

An easy way to think about knowledge management is to think in terms of your firm's Book of Knowledge. Knowledge is stored in employees' heads, in computers, and in reports on the shelf. Additional knowledge pours into the firm on a daily basis from a variety of sources including lessons learned from projects, articles in the daily paper, conferences employees attend, research studies the firm conducts or can access, etc. Knowledge needs to be archived, distilled, and then dispersed in various vehicles for your audience. All of this knowledge—that which is currently in the firm and all that will come into the firm in the future—can be stored in your Book of Knowledge in a way that facilitates easy retrieval and makes it readily available for use with your audience. You will discover through your research that your clients and prospects are paying attention to certain media and you will learn how to reach them via those vehicles in the most convincing way.

The knowledge in your firm will ultimately be structured in a way that gives you ready access to relevant, applicable data and associated graphic materials. When press releases, speeches, or interviews are on the agenda, you will have topical facts and figures at your disposal. Your knowledge, as it is disseminated by your firm, becomes a marketing tool at two levels: first, by building awareness of the firm's expertise and second, by creating a position in the minds of your clients and prospects that your firm's employees are the go-to experts. We will dive further into this concept in the next chapter.

> **TIP: YOU AS THE CUSTOMER**
> - Taking on the customer mindset, think about how you are reached.
> - What grabs you?
> - What makes you decide to purchase?
> - Look at successful marketing and borrow from effective campaigns.

CONCEPT: CRYSTALLIZE KNOWLEDGE INTO STORY IDEAS

The world may not be interested in your entire Book of Knowledge, but your research will point out the specific information your audience *is* interested in and the ways you can effectively share that information. As you review the knowledge that you currently possess, we will show you how to distill that knowledge into story ideas. We use a standard publicity term, "story ideas," to describe any idea that will capture the attention of your audience: an innovative design, a national trend that the firm supports, new research, etc. We will suggest developing Story Idea Archives (and Image Archives), which will provide you with easy access to information that is appropriate for all types of communication, from digital communications to newsletters to press releases. See Chapter Five, Positioning, for more about Story Ideas.

CONCEPT: BRAND YOUR DESIGNERS AS CELEBRITIES

Along with knowledge, another of your greatest assets is your employees. What we refer to as celebrity gets at a key point in marketing a professional services firm and that is the marketing of specific employees and their expertise. Establishing employees as celebrities is one of the goals we suggest you work into your plan. By putting a spotlight on the specific expertise of your employees, you will be personally branding individuals, not just your firm. Imagine a conversation in which a prospect asks someone in the community for the name of the person who can build the state-of-the-art hospital facility and the instant response is the name of one of your employees. This does not happen by chance. It is the result of planning and appropriate dissemination of critical information to your public. In Chapter Two, we talk further about celebrity.

CONCEPT: USE CHEMISTRY TO WIN WORK

Another key point about seeing employees as one of your greatest assets is chemistry. A decision maker at a large medical facility once told us that he found that the designers who responded to the hospital's requests for proposals had an appropriate level of expertise. We asked what influenced his decision regarding which firm to bring on board and he told us that the criteria he used was the chemistry between the hospital team and the design team. In the post interview meeting, he always asked his staff, "Do we want to spend the next few years with this design team?" Conversely, it is important that the design team feels the positive influence of chemistry as they work together and as they establish relationships with prospects and clients. As with celebrity, we talk further about this in Chapter Two.

CONCEPT: MARKET IN CONCENTRIC CIRCLES

An easy and helpful way to think about marketing is concentric circles. As you think about growing your business, whether just starting out or well-established, imagine doing business first with your friendliest contacts and those closest to home—the inner circle. Then, as your client base expands, imagine venturing beyond home and your closest contacts and out into the second concentric circle, all the while maintaining a hold on your inner circle as you develop the outer circle. You can apply the concept geographically; for example, start in Boston, move out to New England, then to the Northeast. Or you can think about it in terms of vertical markets and expanding from one to the other. Either way, the concept of concentric circles will help you assess where you are in your firm's growth. See Chapter Four, Assessment and Analysis, for more information on this concept.

CONCEPT: RANK YOUR PROSPECTS ON THE COURTSHIP CONTINUUM

In the world of fundraising, it is not uncommon to rank prospective donors by "temperature." Stating how cold or warm prospective donors are at a certain point in the fundraising process is the clue to how close they are to becoming a donor. Another way to do the same kind of ranking of prospects is to think in terms of courtship. By using the courtship continuum, we attempt to gauge where the relationship with a prospect stands and what the next strategy is for turning that prospect into a new client.

More specifically, if signing a contract can be seen as getting to the altar, then we can back up and see that in order to achieve that goal, we have to become engaged, and before that we have to go on several dates, and before that we have to ask someone out on a first date, and before that we have to meet the person, and before that we have to identify who that person is! In Chapter Four, Assessment and Analysis, we talk further about this as a way of assessing prospects.

CONCEPT: RANK YOUR PROSPECTS BY FOLLOWING THE MONEY

The highest priority of your marketing efforts is to find people with cash who will turn it over to your company. Sounds obvious, but it bears comment. We tell our students and clients to take the "Deep Throat" approach from the film *All the President's Men* and "follow the money." Nonprofit fundraisers are quite familiar with this way of thinking and we propose that for-profit businesses should be just as comfortable with the concept. In upcoming chapters, research and industry trends will help you define your target markets and their needs and how to position your firm to capture clients and meet their needs.

CONCEPT: MARKET TO ONE VERTICAL MARKET AT A TIME

The firm-wide marketing plan that we are focused on completing in this book can often seem huge. We recommend that you also consider narrowing your focus and doing a smaller marketing plan for each vertical market. In Chapter Three, Research, we focus on the Vertical Market Worksheet, which will be exactly that—the plan for one market at a time.

CONCEPT: MARKET TO ONE PROSPECT AT A TIME

You can telescope your efforts even further and make great strides if you also think in terms of a mini-marketing plan devised for one prospect at a time. It may sound quite narrow and seem like more work, but we believe that if you rank your prospects according to the courtship continuum, you can then easily isolate the particular strategies you need to move each prospect closer to the altar.

CONCEPT: "I KNOW WHAT YOU WANT AND I'VE GOT IT!"

Although the old pink phone message slips are now dinosaurs, there is a valuable lesson to be learned from them. In our marketing experience, we always imagined our prospect returning from lunch to a pile of a dozen pink phone message slips and we wanted to make sure our call was the one that was returned first. A consultant suggested we shape our message as "I know what you want and I've got it." Not only did that format work for getting phone calls returned, but we suggest it as the structure of your positioning statement. Throughout the book, you will see how we focus on this concept as a marketing advantage.

WHAT LIES AHEAD

Now that we have reviewed these overarching concepts, we will move on to what lies ahead for you as you develop a concrete marketing plan. We recommend that you first read the entire book without doing the exercises. After you have reviewed and absorbed the content of *Business Comes to the Expert,* the process of conducting research, completing the worksheets, archiving your knowledge, and defining your goals and strategies will come more easily.

A summary of the chapters follows. You can anticipate some hard work ahead, but no matter where you are on the spectrum, a one-person firm or a 50-person firm, you will produce a well formulated marketing plan and realize solid results.

Chapter Two - Product or Service: What Are You Selling?

Normally we think of our services and the portfolio of the buildings we have designed as the sum of what we are selling. This chapter introduces the idea of looking at the two greatest assets not listed on your balance sheet: your firm's knowledge and your employees. Managing your knowledge for easy retrieval and dissemination is fundamental to effective marketing. Viewing employees as an asset suggests that the issues of celebrity and chemistry are key to building the awareness of expertise and the relationships necessary to successful marketing. In addition, we introduce the Knowledge Leader—the person responsible for managing your knowledge—and delve into the Book of Knowledge, demonstrating how to categorize the information you possess.

Chapter Three – Market Research: Marketing to Whom?

In this chapter we cover research methods and where and how you can easily find information about your industry, your vertical markets, your competition, and your prospects and clients. Deciding who you want as clients is the first step. Learning how you are perceived, learning what challenges clients and prospects see on the horizon, and determining how they want to be communicated with will allow you to position your firm effectively. Your front-line marketers, your employees, are included in the research process as well. We introduce both the Vertical Market Worksheet and the SCOT Worksheet (strengths, challenges, opportunities, and threats), which you will use as the repository for all that you learn in your research.

Chapter Four - Assessment and Analysis: Where Are You Now?

There is no substitute for that clear-eyed look at your current situation. It is easy for most firms to list their strengths, but embracing what is perceived as negatives can be difficult. We start by introducing methods for ranking your prospects—which will make it easy for you to strategize about moving each one further toward the altar. We also introduce Target Market Effectors so you can assess the awareness and attitude of your audience. More broadly, we introduce the Communications Audit to help you assess the four elements of communication—audience, message, vehicle, and frequency—and determine if there are gaps, overlaps, or room for improvement in your communications campaign. Finally, we provide a Publicity Questionnaire to help you assess the current status of your publicity efforts.

Chapter Five - Positioning Your Firm and Your Designers: How Do You Create the Message?

Now it is time to take what you have learned in the research about client and prospect needs and match it to your knowledge and expertise to create a message for your audience—a message that differentiates you from your competition and says, "I know what you want and I've got it." You will learn how to bring your knowledge to the marketplace—through the elevator speech, case histories, the testimonials, and the tagline. In short, you are positioning your firm and your employees as the go-to experts. We will show you how ABC Design, and your firm, can translate knowledge and research into the positioning message.

Chapter Six - Goals: Where Do You Want to Go?

Understanding where you want to go means setting achievable goals and spelling out your vision in both narrative and financial form of how you will reach those goals. We will introduce a Goals Worksheet that you will use in later chapters to fill in corresponding strategies and tactics that will finally land in the To-Do List.

Chapter Seven - Tools: How Best to Deliver Your Message?

To determine how you will share your message, we will discuss the management functions and specific tools that come together as the total delivery effort for marketing. We will give guidance on everything from managing your database to using advertising, publicity, direct mail, digital communications, presentations, professional societies, trade shows, and conferences.

Chapter Eight - Strategies: How Will You Get There?

In Chapter Eight, we revisit all the worksheets to pull all strategies from them, ensuring that all strategies are linked to your goals. Then, we help you narrow strategies down to tactics for the To-Do List assignments that will move you steadily toward achieving your goals. We also talk about mini-marketing plans for vertical markets and for single prospects.

Chapter Nine - Staff: Who Will Do the Work?

Here we examine how a marketing team is organized and what percentage of time employees devote to marketing. We clarify the roles and job descriptions, review the levels of leadership devoted to the plan, and discuss getting the entire firm on board for action and results. We will specifically address the expectations for those leading the vertical markets with respect to the ways they will penetrate their respective markets, such as giving speeches and writing columns.

Chapter Ten - The *To Do List*: What is the Schedule?

Now is the time to author your To-Do List with action items, personnel assignments, and deadlines. As a living document that grows and changes as information is gathered and actions are taken, the To-Do List is a usable, efficient tool devised to help you manage the global and daily intricacies of your marketing plan.

Chapter Eleven - Budget: How Much Will it Cost?

In this chapter we discuss creating the marketing budget, including allocating appropriate salary costs, record keeping, sales projections and marketing to sales ratios. We demonstrate the budget that ABC Design has created for itself to carry out the goals and strategies it set as a result of its research.

Chapter Twelve - Evaluation: How Will You Recognize Success?

The measures of success you will want to consider are profitability, satisfied clients, reputation, celebrity employees, awards and peer recognition. We discuss tracking, measuring, and reporting your firm-wide success. And we include information on Post-occupancy Evaluations.

CONCLUSION

It is our intention that, by the end of this book, you will be able to answer the following questions, all of which are the most often asked in our seminars.

- How do we get more visibility? *See Chapter Seven, Tools, and Chapter Eight, Strategies.*

- How do we get to the right audience? *Review your Vertical Market Worksheet in Chapter Three, Market Research, and Chapter Seven, Tools.*

- How do we capture high-quality prospects? *Look at the prospect assessment information in Chapter Four, Assessment and Analysis, and the mini-marketing plan concept in Chapter Eight, Strategies.*

- How do we decide which marketing vehicles will work best for us? *In Chapter Three, Research, you will learn from your client/prospect research what vehicles they are reading, listening to, and watching.*

- How do we get more efficient in our public relations outreach? *Look at Chapter Five, Positioning, for how best to craft your positioning message and story ideas for press releases, and in Chapter Seven, Tools, in which we provide a Publicity Questionnaire to assess your efforts.*

- How do we let people know about the value of our services? How do we choose the most compelling story? *In Chapter Five, Positioning, we discuss how to translate your knowledge into story ideas to capture the attention of your market.*

- How do we move forward if our marketing efforts are not working? *Review Chapter Three, Research and tailor your research questions to inquire fully about what is and is not working; review Target Market Effectors in Chapter Four to see where the problem lies; and revisit your research results to ensure you understand what your market wants, needs and is paying attention to and that you are effectively penetrating that market with your message.*

- How do we create accountability for marketing within the firm? *Review Chapter Nine, Staff.*

- How do we build recognition? *See Chapter, Seven, Tools.*

- How do we create a marketing budget? *See Chapter 11, Budget.*

- How do we measure the effectiveness of our marketing efforts? *See Chapter 12, Evaluation.*

PRODUCT OR SERVICE: WHAT ARE YOU SELLING?

YOUR KNOWLEDGE AND YOUR EMPLOYEES

usiness Comes to the Expert means that if you are known for possessing expertise needed by your audience, your audience will come to you. That is why we believe that marketing starts with knowledge management. It sounds simple, but it requires a concentrated effort of amassing your knowledge and then communicating it to your audience in a way that is comprehensible and meaningful and that highlights your employees as the go-to designers for that expertise. Normally, design firms think of their services and the portfolio of their designs as the sum of what they are selling. In this chapter, we explore the concept of seeing your two greatest assets—your firm's knowledge and your employees—as the essence of what you are selling. First, we will look at your knowledge.

27

FOUNTAIN OF CONTENT

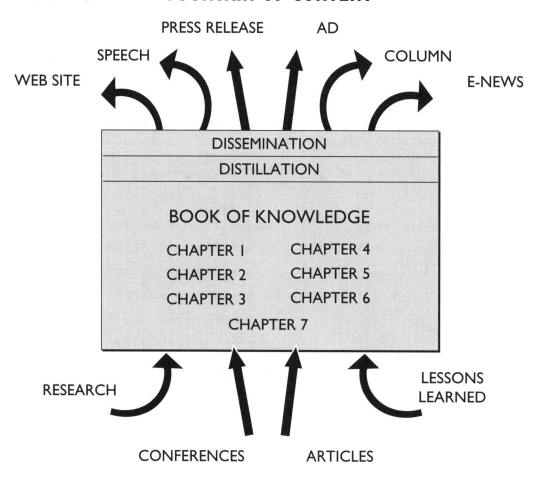

Note: the Book of Knowledge is the central part of the Fountain of Content.

THE FOUNTAIN OF CONTENT AND YOUR BOOK OF KNOWLEDGE

As someone in Hollywood once said, "content is king." Imagine a fountain of content flowing into your organization on a daily basis from endless sources, including lessons learned from projects, in articles in the daily paper; from conferences employees attend, from research studies the firm conducts or can access, etc. Think about all the knowledge your firm already possesses—stored in employees' heads, in computer files, and in reports on shelves. That ever evolving knowledge base is an asset that can ultimately flow out into various communication vehicles (speeches, columns, newsletters, etc.) to your target markets to build awareness of your firm and employees as the go-to experts.

But how do you capture that content as it flows into your organization and how do you transform it into something the market is looking for? The easiest way is to think in terms of your firm's Book of Knowledge. Consider the knowledge you have that sets you apart from your competition and how you would categorize that knowledge. What would you title your firm's Book of Knowledge? What topics would your book address that could be slotted into the book's chapters? Sustainable design, historic preservation, healthcare design, multi-unit housing?

We suggest that you create a Book of Knowledge folder in your computer, with subfolders for each chapter. What are the titles of the chapters that serve to categorize all your knowledge? You can start by categorizing what you currently know. As new information comes into the organization, you will have an appropriate system to not only store but also easily retrieve the data. With this system, confusion and questions about what happens to information when it comes into the firm will be avoided. After listing your chapters and reviewing your entire body of knowledge, you will be able to think about two things: how you currently use your knowledge and how you could use it for more effective results.

The goal is for your Book of Knowledge information to be structured in a way that gives you ready access to relevant, applicable information and associated graphic materials. Then, when press releases, speeches, or interviews are on your agenda, you will have topical data at your immediate disposal and will have identified the employee who can deliver the message.

We believe that the world is probably not interested in your entire Book of Knowledge. In Chapter Three, Market Research, you will learn from your research the specific information your audience is interested in and which communication vehicles your audience is paying attention to so you can use those vehicles to reach them in the most convincing way.

When your knowledge leaves the firm, it becomes a marketing tool at two levels: first, by building awareness of the firm's expertise, and second, by creating a position in the minds of clients and prospects that your employees are the go-to experts for services.

To demonstrate how you can create your Book of Knowledge, title, and chapters, we will take a look at how ABC Design assessed and archived its knowledge. As we mentioned in Chapter One, ABC Design is an urban firm, serving two primary markets, senior living and healthcare, and a secondary market in education. With specialties in historic preservation and sustainability that crossed over all three markets, they named their book of knowledge: "Sustainable Restoration Solutions." The sections and chapters are as follows:

Section A—Senior Living
Chapter 1 Continuing Care Retirement Community Design
Chapter 2 Assisted Living Design
Chapter 3 Master Planning and Building Analysis
Chapter 4 Sustainability
Chapter 5 Accessibility
Chapter 6 Renovation
Chapter 7 Healing and Memory Gardens
Chapter 8 Historic Preservation

Section B—Healthcare
Chapter 1 Sustainability in Healthcare
Chapter 2 Master Planning and Building Analysis
Chapter 3 Imaging Departments
Chapter 4 Renovation/Conversion to High-Tech Imaging Equipment

DISTILLATION

The best place to start with the process of distilling your knowledge is with your case histories—those one sheet, at-a-glance summaries of your projects. They are one of the most important ways to translate your knowledge into meaningful communications for the market. Also referred to as case studies, project histories, project synopses or project closeout reports, they are an encapsulation of the critical elements of a project and pack the most punch when they reflect your brand, include a client testimonial, are contained on a single page, and feature a dynamic photograph.

We recommend that case histories contain the following three elements: the challenge presented by the client, the recommendation presented by your firm, and the successful result that can be reduced to the client testimonial. See Chapter Seven, Tools, for various ways to present case histories. As you look at your case histories, it will be easy to see the features and benefits involved in each project—the feature being what you offered to the client, and the benefit that accrued to the client as a result of the work the firm provided to them.

In addition, case histories and features and benefits are fodder for story ideas for the media, for seminars, columns, press releases, newsletters, and your Web site. Story ideas can range from an innovative design for a building to a national trend your firm brought to the local market or a solution to a thorny problem.

All of the knowledge about your firm can be further condensed into an elevator speech. An elevator speech is a technique in which you have approximately 30 seconds, or the duration of an elevator ride, to inform or persuade someone about your service or product.

Finally, you can distill your key information into a tagline—a brief, evocative slogan or phrase that conveys the most important attribute or benefit of your company, product, or service that you wish to convey. Taglines are generally used as a theme to a campaign. Familiar examples include: Dell Computer's "Easy as Dell;" Verizon's "We never stop working for you;" and Newman's Own "Shameless exploitation in pursuit of the common good." (All taglines are the trademarks or service marks of their respective owners.)

In Chapter Five, Positioning, we will look further at how to distill your Book of Knowledge into smaller, manageable, and newsworthy bits of information, including your mission statement, case histories, story ideas for the media, your elevator speech, and your tagline. These condensed messages are all used in various ways to interest your audience, whether client, prospect, or reporter.

DISSEMINATION

Now you are ready to disseminate the knowledge to your vertical markets through speaking and writing opportunities. In Chapter Seven, Tools, we will fully discuss how designated employees will be positioned as the experts, the go-to people on particular topics with the goal that when clients and prospects need expertise, your firm and the experts within will come to mind first. We are reminded of a column written by a colleague a few years ago that featured a catchy title, was focused on the latest advances in pediatric care and appeared in a regional medical newsletter. Shortly after it appeared in print, she visited a regional hospital to solicit business and, to her surprise, one of the doctors at the conference table pulled out the article and praised her insight. As you progress through all the processes in this book to develop and then execute your marketing plan, we hope you ultimately enjoy a similar experience.

THE PERSON IN CHARGE

It may seem obvious but it bears mentioning that in the most effective systems one person is in charge. We refer to the person in charge of your knowledge management as your Knowledge Leader. You may refer to this person as your Director of Marketing. The Knowledge Leader/Director of Marketing is the person in charge of your firm-wide knowledge who knows the breadth of the information in your Book of Knowledge and how to retrieve it for easy dissemination.

Your Knowledge Leader must know how your knowledge is currently being used to market the firm and must then manage the marketing to build awareness of your firm in the marketplace via the vehicles your prospects and clients are paying attention to, listening to, and reading. We talk more about responsibilities and job descriptions for a typical marketing staff in Chapter Nine, Staff.

VERTICAL MARKETS

Before we do more with the Book of Knowledge, we need to continue to set the stage concerning your knowledge base. We begin with vertical markets, which are defined as a particular industry or group of enterprises in which similar products or services are developed and marketed using similar methods. In the broad arena of the design industry, senior living, education, housing, and healthcare are examples of distinct vertical markets. Within each of those markets are special divisions or sub-markets. For example, senior living can be broken down into independent living, assisted living, and nursing care.

Once you have identified a vertical market as a potential for your firm, you can use pertinent resources within that vertical market to find out about trends and about the various building projects and design needs within the market. That information is available to you through a variety of resources. You can contact the professional society that serves a vertical market and read the periodicals produced by and for that market. For example, to gather information on the higher education market, peruse the Society for College and University Planning Web site at *www.scup.org* or read the *Chronicle of Higher Education*.

NAME YOUR VERTICAL MARKET LEADERS

The next level of knowledge leadership is the Vertical Market Leader, usually a principal or an associate, who will manage the knowledge associated with a specific market, who possesses concentrated knowledge and expertise in that market, and who will be tasked with speaking and writing on assigned topics. Assigning vertical market leaders will increase your ability to build a market presence.

CELEBRITY AND CHEMISTRY

We believe that the extent to which an organization performs well will largely depend on how effectively its employees absorb new knowledge, share knowledge throughout the organization, and use knowledge to its best effect when imparting it to target markets. This is the key to building awareness in the marketplace of your designers as the go-to experts or celebrities. Again, imagine that conversation in which a prospect asks someone in the community for the name of the person who can provide a specific design solution and the instant response is your name or that of an employee. An additional and interesting aspect of the conversation is that the answer to the question was not just the name of your design firm or the name of the specific department within your firm focused on designing hospitals but rather the person—the Vertical Market Leader—who heads up that initiative. That is the result of successful personal branding, where, through knowledge management, you have built employee celebrity.

The intangible element of good chemistry is credited by many clients as adding to the success of their projects. As you are establishing the celebrity of each Vertical Market Leader, you must also be aware of individual working styles and personality traits and be alert to forming teams that work well together within the firm and with clients. As we stated earlier, once your prospects are convinced that your design team has the expertise they are seeking, they will look next at whether or not they feel comfortable with you and want to spend the next few years in a day-to-day working relationship with you. It is difficult to give particular tips on building chemistry, but we do know that prior to prospect meetings, designers discuss chemistry-related concerns such as the layout of the meeting room, whether to bring audio-visuals or not, what to wear, etc. You will have your own take on how to ensure that the chemistry is right. We simply mention it as a reminder of its importance.

FEATURES AND BENEFITS

Knowledge and employees are your key assets, but they are not the only assets to consider when using knowledge management as the basis of your marketing. The point of marketing is to find clients: those people who are fun and interesting to work with and who have the financial resources that will support your corporate goals. As prospects become aware of your firm and your employees, they will evaluate your portfolio, your philosophy, awards, media coverage, and even your work space. They will also evaluate chemistry and charisma and will be specifically looking for the benefits you bring to a working relationship.

To arrive at the benefits you bring to the table, it is helpful to first look at features. Features describe and define the aspects of your product or service, while benefits define how life will improve for your client. Of the two, what clients care about most are benefits. The best way to look at the difference between features and benefits is by example. In its marketing materials, a famous men's chorus minimally promotes its feature: singing. Instead, it promotes the benefits it offers: communal spirit, community involvement, and personal pride. The Health and Safety Program at a local Red Cross chapter teaches CPR, its feature, but the benefit promoted is helping people lead safer, healthier lives through education and training. The ability to design specific building types is the feature you offer to clients. The benefit may be the use of materials that guarantee a longer life for the building and substantial savings on long-term maintenance.

As you create your case histories and state the three key elements—the challenge presented by the client, the recommendation presented by your firm (the feature), and the result (the benefit)—you will be

• Assign the responsibility to the Knowledge Leader and marketing team to establish and update Book of Knowledge folders.
• Share communication messages with employees first so the entire staff is aware of and familiar with the messages that will be shared with a firm's audiences.
• Set up computers with shared drive public files so employees have access to the knowledge base. (The shared drive should be in read-only format so information can be viewed and printed but not altered. Only specifically named employees will have privileges to update Book of Knowledge folders.)

clarifying the features and benefits of each of your projects. The benefits will be enormously helpful to you as you create your positioning message in Chapter Five.

CONCLUSION

By now, you have come up with the title and chapter names of your firm's Book of Knowledge and have begun to sort your knowledge into it. At the minimum, start the process by at least noting in your Book of Knowledge where different information can be easily found. You have clarified your vertical markets. You have confirmed your Knowledge Leader/Director of Marketing, who will be committed to tracking your firm's knowledge and managing the marketing plan. And you have confirmed the leaders of your vertical markets who have agreed to be the disseminators of your firm knowledge by writing and speaking on topics of interest to their vertical markets. Now we are ready to move forward to Chapter Three, which is chock-full of all things research.

MARKET RESEARCH: MARKETING TO WHOM?

BENEFITS OF RESEARCH

In this chapter, you will dive into research and get acquainted with the two tools you will use to track what you will learn during the research process: the Vertical Market Worksheet, which is a great at-a-glance look at both your smaller plan for each vertical market and your entire firm-wide marketing plan; and the SCOT Worksheet, which covers the strengths, challenges, opportunities, and threats that you will uncover in your research interviews. These worksheets will be two of the key sources for the strategies you will use to build your marketing plan. In upcoming chapters, you will see other sources of strategies, from assessment methods in Chapter Four to the Goals Worksheet in Chapter Six.

Before beginning the actual research tasks, take a moment to think about some of the benefits of research. First, research provides critical knowledge to your firm from outside sources, information that will be added to knowledge you already possess. (You can see that research is a source for that Fountain of Content we already mentioned.) Second, it is good to remember that although you may think of research in terms of the questions you are asking, in fact, it is also a great opportunity to market your firm by educating respondents about your capabilities. Third, research is a chance to learn if there are projects the interviewee needs taken care of immediately that may provide you with a perfect opportunity for quick project turnaround. Fourth, research is an opportunity for you to have your assumptions challenged. We have found that it is not infrequent for firms to find that what *they* think are their greatest strengths are not always what *their clients* think are their greatest strengths. Fifth, research is a chance to learn about a negative that you were not aware of but are capable of remedying. And sixth, although we often think of research as a process that is conducted once a year for the marketing plan, it really should be categorized as a daily task. Obviously, the kind of formal client/prospect interviews we are talking about in this chapter will be conducted only once a year, but having your radar up and being open to new knowledge on a daily basis is critical. Valuable information is always available, you just need to gather it and act on it.

WHAT DO YOU NEED TO KNOW?

It may sound obvious but it is worth mentioning that before conducting research, it is good to look at what you want to learn. It is easy to get lost in research—there is a wealth of information out there —but is it what you need to know? Consider the questions you need answered in order to fill out the worksheets we provide in this chapter. By answering key questions, you begin the process of effectively positioning your firm in your vertical markets. The following questions will help you identify what is working in your marketing efforts, as well as what needs to be revised or added.

- Whom do you want as clients?
- Are the vertical markets you are working in thriving?
- What trends are occurring in your vertical markets?
- What do your clients and prospects think of your firm? Of your strengths and challenges?
- What do your clients or prospects want or need?
- What challenges are they facing today?
- What do they see on their horizon that will require design assistance?
- What do your clients or prospects read, watch, listen to, belong to, or attend? (This will tell you what you should be paying attention to and how you can best reach them.)
- What means of communication do they favor: e-mail, phone, meetings?
- Who are your competitors and how are they successfully marketing?
- What do you consider to be successful marketing? What can you learn from successful marketing in comparison to what you are doing now?
- In which professional societies should you participate?
- In which trade conferences or seminars should you participate?
- Who influences your prospects? Are you marketing to these influencers?
- How are you reached? What do you like about the marketing campaigns that are focused on you? What makes you decide to purchase?
- Do you effectively analyze and utilize your research?

"I KNOW WHAT YOU WANT AND I'VE GOT IT."

The most important message to deliver to prospects and clients is the phrase, "I know what you want and I've got it." With the notion that all strategy will spring forth from your goals and your research, in this chapter we cover research methods and where and how you can find information about your industry, your competition, your prospects and clients and, specifically, what your prospects and clients are seeking. Learning this will allow you to say with credibility: "I know what you want." By determining the vertical markets in which your design team can satisfy recognized needs that are the most interesting and compatible with your skill set (*and* that will be profitable), you will be able to promote your knowledge, expertise, and strengths more effectively within each market as well as differentiate yourself from other firms in the same market. That will allow you to say with authority the second half of that sentence: "I've got it."

Research is defined as a critical, thorough investigation, so prepare to devote the time and resources required to obtain helpful results. In addition to learning how your firm is perceived, you will want to learn about the challenges your clients and prospects face now and the challenges they see on their business horizons that could be opportunities for you to serve them. Understanding your clients' needs and potential for growth or change will have a direct influence on your ability to capture future work with them. We are assuming that you will perform your own research, but many firms, small, medium, and large, contract the research process out to consultants who specialize in market research. Because research is so critical to effective marketing, some of the large national and multi-national design firms support a dedicated research staff within their marketing departments. However you decide to do it, you will want to do the kind of annual research that feeds your annual plan, and at the same time, you will want to think about research as a daily commitment.

Once you have completed all the research to include in your annual plan, you will combine it with your Book of Knowledge information, and you will be able to "walk the walk" by confidently telling prospects that you not only understand the issues they are confronting, but you have experience providing solutions.

THE VERTICAL MARKET WORKSHEET

The completed Vertical Market Worksheet is a great way to put your marketing plan into visual form since it provides an at-a-glance look both at the entire marketing plan and smaller vertical market plans. The worksheet is provided as a tool to lay out the information needed to effectively market to existing and potential vertical markets. It covers your firm's history in your markets, your activity in associated professional societies, your depth of networking relationships, and the vehicles you use for disseminating knowledge.

The first exercise with this worksheet, *before* you conduct any research, is to fill it out as a team using information from your historical records and current market activities. Then you will be able to easily see where you need to conduct research to fill in the gaps. Once all research is completed, add the information discovered during your research that embellishes what you have already incorporated into the worksheet—whether about projections, prospects, competition, influencers, vehicles, etc. In the case of a prospective market, you may find that you are more than ready to compete in that market or that it is not a good knowledge match at this time. (To save time and effort for exercises in upcoming chapters, save your completed worksheets because we will revisit and reuse the basic information.)

Use the blank Vertical Market Worksheet that follows for your firm. Use the completed ABC Design worksheet that follows (filled in with information possessed prior to and after the research process) as a guideline. (This and all other worksheets illustrated in this book are available online at: *www.greenway. us/expertbook*).

WORKSHEET INSTRUCTIONS

The information required for insertion in the Vertical Market Worksheet comes from your research. The worksheet is laid out with vertical markets listed across the top and research topics running down the left column. Add or subtract research topics to satisfy your particular need to know, and add rows to accommodate all the information you want to detail for each topic. Following is a brief description of each line item.

- **Vertical Market Leader**: Name your in-house leader. This person should have the most knowledge and be the most experienced in working in the specific market. Depending on the size of your firm, you can list additional professionals who are working in the vertical market. (Employees may be named in more than one vertical market.)

- **Further Definition**: When possible, markets should be broken down. For example, senior living can be broken down into independent living, assisted living, and nursing care.

Vertical Market Worksheet			
	Primary Market 1 - Senior Living	Primary Market 2 - Healthcare	Secondary Market 1 - Education
Vertical Market Leader			
Further Definition			
Industry Projections			
Firm Profitability in Market			
• Historical Profit			
• Projected Profit			
Knowledge			
Portfolio			
Current Clients			
Prospects			
Influencers			
Partners			
Competition			
Vehicles:			
• Professional Society Memberships			
• Media to Listen to, Read, Watch			
• Conferences/Trade Shows			
• Writing/Speaking Opportunities			
• Award Opportunities			

See: www.greenway.us/expertbook for this template

- **Industry Projections**: Include national and regional growth trends and forecasts for each market.

- **Firm Profitability in Market**: Historical profit is a record of your firm's historical data of gross revenues and profitability in each market. Projected profit is an estimate of your firm's projected revenue and profitability per market.

- **Knowledge**: List your expertise and note it as "extensive," "competent," or "need more knowledge." If more knowledge is needed, make a note of strategies you will need for attaining. We will discuss further action on strategies in Chapter Eight.

- **Portfolio**: Briefly note if you have projects from this market in your portfolio or if you need to take photographs and produce case histories with testimonials.

- **Current Clients**: List clients with active projects.

- **Prospects**: Rank prospects by using the Courtship Continuum. (See Chapter Four regarding assessments).

- **Influencers**: List owners, consultants, developers, facilities managers—those people in your database who have influence in the market you are researching and with whom you will want to communicate.

- **Partners**: List consultants, vendors, and others that you partner with in the teaming process.

- **Competition**: List significant players, whether local, regional, or national.

The remaining line items in the worksheet address how you connect with your vertical market and reinforce the data gathering that tells you what your clients, prospects, and influencers are reading, listening to, and watching as well as which vehicles you can use to communicate with them.

- **Professional Society Memberships**: Select organizations your Vertical Market Leaders will participate in, and secure memberships. (Adjust budget for annual dues.)

- **Media to Listen To, Read, and Watch**: List media options in which you should place articles or be heard or seen and record deadlines for copy or appearances. Determine subscriptions and discuss possible advertisements. (Budget costs.)

- **Conferences/Trade Shows**: Select conferences to attend, budget the cost of participation, and select participants. (Tip: Upon learning of a conference, you may choose not to attend given budget constraints, but note the conference on the worksheet with a "no go" annotation and track it for insertion in the budget for the coming year or when your budget will allow.)

- **Writing/Speaking Opportunities**: Research what opportunities are afforded for speaking engagements by professional societies and local business organizations along with opportunities for writing columns for professional society newsletters and even your local newspaper. Determine which employees will write columns and fulfill speaking engagements. Determine topics and venues from your research. (Add travel costs to your budget.)

- **Award Opportunities**: Select award programs for participation and record upcoming deadlines. (Add application fees and production expenses such as graphic design and photography to the budget.)

Vertical Market Worksheet ABC Design			
	Primary Market 1 - Senior Living	Primary Market 2 - Healthcare	Secondary Market 1 - Education
Vertical Market Leader	Ann Forest	Dan Lane	Mike Branch
Further Definition NOTE: All markets = sustainability, accessibility, master planning, cost analysis	Encompasses Independent Living, Assisted, Nursing and Dementia Units	Hospitals with specialty in high tech Imaging Units, renovation, medical clinics	Secondary Education, Renovation
Industry Projections	Continuing steady growth for aging population in this region	Continuing steady growth for aging population in this region	Mandates for updated facilities statewide
Firm Profitability in Market			
• Historical Profit	10%	10%	
• Projected Profit NOTE: Parlay experience into higher profit margin	20% (10% increase this year.)	20% (10% increase this year.)	12%
Knowledge	Extensive	Extensive	Team: extensive in high tech and renovation. Mike: extensive in education.
Portfolio	Up to date	Up to date	Develop

50

Vertical Market Worksheet ABC Design			
Current Clients	-Eden Retirement -Beacon Sr. Living	-Local Hospital Renovation -County Hospital, new addition -Ames MRI Clinic -Ames MRI (2) -Carroll MRI	
Prospects	Regional Developer Non-profit Dev.	-Conrad Hospital -Dane Clinic -Sussex Hospital	-Ames Secondary Reno -Carroll Secondary Reno
Influencers	Members of Boards Facilities Managers	Facilities Managers	School Board Members Parent Associations Facil ities Managers
Partners	Consultants Vendors	Consultants Vendors	Consultants Vendors
Vehicles:			
• Professional Society Memberships	ALFA, AHCA	ALFA, AHCA	APPA ** Add one membership
• Media to Listen To, Read, Watch	Local media, regional and national pubs	Local media, regional and national pubs	Local, regional media National pubs
• Conferences/Trade	2 Regional	2 Regional	1 Statewide

Following is a short list of professional societies that serve and promote designers and their vertical markets. These organizations are sources of diverse information, including national and regional forecasts. See *www.greenway.us/expertbook* for additional resources

American Council of Engineering Companies (ACEC): *www.acec.org*
American Healthcare Association (AHCA): *www.ahca.org*
American Institute of Architects (AIA): *www.aia.org*
American Institute of Constructors (AIC): *www.aicnet.org*
American Seniors Housing Association (ASHA): *www.seniorshousing.org*
American Society of Interior Designers (ASID): *www.asid.org*
APPA Serving Educational Facilities Professionals (APPA): *www.appa.org*
Assisted Living Facilities Association (ALFA): *www.alfa.org*
Associated General Contractors of America (AGC): *www.agc.org*
Centers for Medicaid and Medicare Services: *www.cms.hhs.gov/NationalHealthExpendData*
College Planning and Management Magazine (CPM): *www.peterli.com/cpm*
Construction Specifications Institute (CSI): *www.csinet.org*
Dodge Analytics: *www.dodge.construction.com/analytics*
Engineering News Record (ENR): *www.enr.construction.com*
International Interior Design Association (IIDA): *www.iida.com*
Lodging Econometrics: *www.lodgingeconometrics.com*
National Association of Independent Schools (NAIS): *www.nais.org*
National Health Expenditure Data: United States Department of Health & Human Services/
 National Multi Housing Council (NMHC): *www.nmhc.org*
PriceWaterhouseCoopers HealthCast 2010: *www.pwc.com*
School Planning and Management Magazine (SPM): *www.peterli.com/spm*
Society for Marketing Professional Services (SMPS): *www.smps.org*
Society for College and University Planning (SCUP): *www.scup.org*

INDUSTRY RESEARCH

In this section, we are looking at the vertical markets, but first, we will back up and take a look at the entire industry. It is helpful to review what industry icons report. For example, the American Institute of Architects learned in a recent study about the public's perceptions of the profession and what the public sees as the critical benefit of working with an architect. The positive perceptions included: multi-talented professionals who are well educated, knowledgeable individuals who are organized, think strategically, and see the big picture. The negative perceptions included: difficult or fixated on their own creative ideas; lose sight of their client's organizational objectives and budget needs; do not listen well; and have their own agenda. In short, the respondents want an architect to fully understand the client's perspective on a project before starting work. The respondents did see the benefit of working with an architect: They said it was exciting and creative, they liked a strong relationship and the guidance; they felt that the architect's vision added a valuable dimension and reality to their own vision; they loved the promise of superior results; and they felt that using an architect created an expectation of more livable and useful environments. So how can we sum up what the market is looking for in an architect? One who is an expert, who listens, minimizes risk, solves problems, provides distinguished design, is trustworthy, likeable and uses technology to benefit the project.

Now, we narrow our focus to the vertical markets. Each vertical market is represented by professional associations and there are a variety of easily accessible resources, some of which we have listed, that provide invaluable industry information from trends, to economic statistics, to demographics, to leaders within the industry. For example, the American Institute of Architects provides an online newsletter that includes updates on trends and industry forecasts. You can read industry publications, ask current clients, join professional associations, contact news sources, and visit Internet sites and the local library to find answers to questions.

The industry information you are looking for includes growth of the overall economy, movement within a particular vertical market, upcoming national trends, and significant funding, whether public or private sector, that will spawn construction. In the public sector, for example, a national highway bill may potentially generate commercial construction such as office parks, shopping malls, and multi-unit housing, and changes in state and local budgets may produce municipal contracts and school construction over an extended period.

Understanding trends in your markets—the ups and the downs—and then understanding how trends will directly affect your bottom line is a critical part of the marketing process. If a certain market is threatened by a downturn, you need to be aware and have a plan in place to divest yourself of that market and replace it or expand in another market. Whether your markets are local, regional, or national, you will want to be aware of trends in each area in order to be recession-proof. You will want to be prepared to broaden or narrow your market to match predicted trends. You will want to be aware of industry trends to avoid projecting an increase in a vertical market that is declining, and you will want to be able to relay and discuss trends with clients in a knowledgeable manner.

NOTE: While general information about the industry, such as growth projections, can be included in the Vertical Market Worksheet, you will want to incorporate specific industry trends into the SCOT Worksheet either as Opportunities or Threats, depending on which is appropriate.

COMPETITIVE RESEARCH

At the end of the day, you want to compare yourself to your competition in order to make the most informed decisions to improve your firm and gain a competitive advantage. The steps to complete the research on your competition are as follows:

- **Identify**: Determine the identity of your competition. Name the various firms operating in your selected markets in your geographical area.

- **Gather:** Use the numerous sources of information—from the Internet to professional societies, from business publications to your professional colleagues—to gather information about competitions' key players and key projects.

- **Analyze:** Review competitors' Web sites and advertisements. Do they refer to a new service or a new client? A new direction? Are they advertising in a new medium? Are they pitching what makes them unique? How do you compare?

NOTE: While we recommend adding the names of competitors to your Vertical Market Worksheet, you will want to include competitive research information in the SCOT Worksheet as either Opportunities or Threats, whichever is more appropriate.

- Determine the list of clients, prospects, and employees you want to interview. Keep in mind that a smaller number, say, no more than 20 to 30 total, is more manageable and more apt to be completed.
- Confirm that those you interview are incorporated into your database.
- Determine the specific information you want to know about those you interview so you can craft your questions to get focused answers. (Review the list of key questions provided in this chapter.)
- For questions where the answer is potentially a simple yes or no, prepare follow-up questions to pose during the interview to gather more complete information.
- Send an e-mail or appropriate inquiry asking for a phone appointment and state how much time you will need (15 to 20 minutes is ideal).
  - o E-mail message to send clients to arrange an appointment for research:

    "I have been retained to assist ABC Design in preparing its marketing strategy for the coming year. As a valued client, your opinions are important and will help the company serve you better. I have questions that will take about 20 minutes to answer. Could we arrange a phone appointment to talk? If you wish, your responses will be confidential."
  - o E-mail message to send prospects to arrange an appointment for research:

    "I am representing ABC Design, an architectural design firm specializing in historic preservation and sustainable projects in senior living, healthcare, and education. The company is preparing its marketing strategy for the coming year and would like to ask you a few questions that will assist them with their planning. I have questions that will take about 20 minutes to answer. Could we arrange a phone appointment to talk? If you wish, your responses will be confidential."
- Be prepared to type or tape (with permission) responses.

CLIENT RESEARCH

In client research, important questions to answer are, "What do your clients want?" "What challenges are they facing?" and "What do clients think of your firm, including employees and services offered?" Since your goals within your marketing plan are to retain good clients and find new ones, the best way to do that is to understand if you are performing well for your current clients. Study the suggested client questions, and use them during the interview to gain the client's perspective on individuals within your firm and on the value your clients place on the work your firm is providing. Do not be afraid to ask what you might perceive as a difficult question because the information gathered from client research is the most valuable in promoting your strengths to the marketplace. In the case of discovering negatives, you gain the opportunity to address and improve in those areas. In our experience with the interview process, we have found clients and prospects to be very cooperative in participating in the process, particularly if we adhered to the stated amount of time required.

In marketing to clients and prospects, you need to learn what they expect to be facing in the future and if they would be interested in the expertise your firm offers that addresses those issues. Then you can communicate to them your ability to address and satisfy their needs. Beyond learning about what your clients and prospects read, watch, and listen to, you want to learn how clients like to be communicated with and, therefore, how they want to hear from you. Because you must use the most effective means to make a positive and lasting impression, learn whether they prefer e-mail, letters, newsletters, personal contact, or a combination of some or all. When this is determined, you can establish the most effective communications campaign to share your achievements and successes.

Your research will answer questions about the effectiveness of your current marketing efforts. You will discover which efforts are working best to get your desired marketing message out to clients, and you can determine how to change particular efforts for better effect. It is not unusual to learn that what *you* think is your firm's greatest strength is not what *your clients* think is your greatest strength. You may discover some surprising perceptions that will force you to think about how the firm might need to improve what it is doing. Accepting comments about what is not working will lead you in the direction of getting each aspect of your operations and marketing on track.

Documenting the perception of your firm's performance is not a one-time event. Completing thorough, formal client research is a key component to keeping your marketing plan on track, and we propose that if your fiscal year is on a calendar year, you complete client research in late summer or early fall so you can craft your plan through the late fall and early winter for implementation in January. In addition to formal annual research, informal client research is project-driven and may occur more frequently as your project managers and Vertical Market Leaders stay tuned to client perception and satisfaction on a daily basis. Ongoing discussions at the completion of project phases and the compilation of post-occupancy evaluations at project end will cull information that helps improve the knowledge base of the firm. Make project documentation a part of the normal course of business as it will provide invaluable lessons learned.

NOTE: Some of what you learn from your interviews will be inserted into the Vertical Market Worksheet, such as which media outlets and professional societies respondents pay attention to, and some of what you learn will be best inserted into the SCOT Worksheet, such as when you learn a client perception of your firm, you will list that information either as a Strength or a Challenge. If you happen to learn of a particular project they are seeking assistance with, insert details into the Opportunities column.

CLIENT INTERVIEWS

When conducting interviews, it is important to focus on the questions that are pertinent to that person and to keep the interview to the promised amount of time. If your staff has the expertise and time to conduct and analyze research interviews, put them on task or hire a consultant who can meet your needs. A good point to remember in conducting these interviews is that although ostensibly this is all about gathering information from your clients, it is also an opportunity for you or your consultant to educate clients even further about your firm.

A sample of interview questions for clients that you can review and adjust to your needs.
1. How did you hear of ABC Design?
2. What services are covered in your current (or past) contract with the firm? (You, of course, have this information, but you may wish to hear from clients what they think they contracted for.)
3. What qualities are you seeking in a design firm?
4. Why did you choose ABC Design over another firm?
5. What do you perceive as the services they offer?
6. Does ABC Design keep you up-to-date on other services they offer beyond what they are providing for you now? How do you typically hear about these services?
7. How would you like the firm to communicate information about new staff or changes in services,

methods, or technologies that would be beneficial to you: in person, by e-mail, or by direct mail? (This question allows you to accomplish several goals. You let clients know that you have knowledge that is beneficial to them; you ask them what communication methods they prefer; and you ask them for permission to send information.)

8. What do you see on the horizon in your industry that ABC Design firm could assist you with?

9. What do you see as ABC Design's greatest strengths?

10. How does ABC Design's contract price compare with industry standard charges for similar services?

11. What are ABC Design's greatest challenges? What can they improve on to serve you better?

12. Would you contract with them again?

13. What other design firms have you contracted with? Why did you select them?

14. What differentiates ABC Design from other firms?

   (Share with the client: "Just three more questions.")

15. The firm would like to use your positive comments as testimonials in promotional literature. Can I e-mail a consent form to you? (If clients do not want their name used, ask if you could use the testimonial anonymously. Not as good a result, but still helpful.)

16. What do you read, watch, listen to, belong to, and attend?

17. *And now, last question.* Are there any further comments you wish to share with ABC Design?

SCOT: STRENGTHS, CHALLENGES, OPPORTUNITIES, THREATS

The Vertical Market Worksheet gives you an overview of your market activities. In contrast, the SCOT Worksheet that we are now introducing (developed from the traditional strategic tool referred to as the SWOT analysis, exchanging "challenge" for "weakness" to promote a more positive approach to areas that may demand improvement or change) gives you an in-depth view of your organization and the impression the public has of you. This worksheet is the stage in your planning that helps you focus on the key issues referred to as internal factors, strengths and challenges, and external factors, opportunities and threats. In Chapter Eight, we revisit this Worksheet and develop strategies.

WORKSHEET INSTRUCTIONS

Strengths, challenges, opportunities, and threats are standard corporate assessment tools. We have selected our list of categories (running down the left column) from our experience in the design industry and feel that they are the essential pieces of information you need to understand to put your marketing plan together. However, you may want to add or subtract categories.

The information on the Vertical Market Worksheet is based on your internal assessment. The information noted on the SCOT Worksheet is based on the external assessment of clients and prospects that you gather from client/prospect research. Filling out the SCOT Worksheet will most likely take you in two directions. You will further understand how you are doing singularly, and from respondent comments, you will see how you are doing in comparison to your competition.

SCOT Worksheet				
	Strengths	Challenges	Opportunites	Threats
Depth of knowledge				
Scope of services				
Communication skills				
Leadership				
Team structure				
Fees				
Portfolio				
Promotional package				
Proposals				

See: www.greenway.us/expertbook for this template

During the client or prospect interviews, you may learn that clients or prospects have short-term tasks they need assistance with immediately. Since carrying out those tasks could highlight your expertise and your ability to get things done, be sure to follow up on these opportunities ASAP. This way, you are not only using the interview process to gather information but also to obtain work from current clients and prospects.

PROSPECT RESEARCH

The focus of prospect research is to uncover a need your firm can fill, and at the same time, the research process serves as a tool to educate prospects about who you are. By asking prospects about upcoming projects and about the challenges they are facing, you have the opportunity to market the services provided by your firm that directly address their project and solve their design challenge, just as you do with existing clients. Because the goal is to bring prospects in as current clients, you will see that the list of questions for prospects is very similar to the questions prepared for clients. Edit inquiries to get the answers that will satisfy your needs.

If you are wondering how you will be able to get prospects to agree to interviews, we can tell you that in our experience, clients already had some kind of relationship with the prospects they wanted to interview. With one exception, our clients' prospects agreed to be interviewed and we found their responses to be insightful and helpful. As with the other interviews, if time is limited, edit the number of questions to suit clients' schedules and your needs.

SCOT Worksheet ABC Design				
	Strengths	Challenges	Opportunities	Threats
Depth of Knowledge		"Firm is not tracking knowledge to best effect."		
Scope of Services			Staff cited by client as good problem solvers.	
Communication Skills		Audience not aware of firm's entire knowledge		
Leadership	"Project manager led the entire team very well."			
Design Team	Area award-winning sustainable design			
Fees			Revise (increase) firm wide fee structure	
Portfolio			Client stated, "Your design work is better than you represent."	
Promotional Package				Competition from regional design firms.
Proposals		Marketing efforts are reactive, not proactive.		

A sample of interview questions for prospects:

1. Have you heard of ABC Design?

2. If yes, what impression do you have of their strengths? Their challenges?

3. What is on the horizon in your company (or industry) that ABC Design could help you with?

4. Have you ever contracted with a design firm? If yes, why did you choose the firm?

5. For what projects or services?

6. How did you feel about the experience? (*Probe further about types of services, quality of service, price.*)

7. What are you currently looking for in a design firm?

8. Would you like introductory information about ABC Design?

9. How would you like us to communicate information about new staff or changes in services, methods, or technologies that would be beneficial to you: in person, by e-mail, or by direct mail? (*Share with the client: "Just two more questions."*)

10. What do you read, watch, listen to, belong to, and attend?

11. *And now, last question.* Are there any further comments you wish to share regarding ABC Design?

NOTE: For the prospect research responses, information in questions 9 and 10 will go into the Vertical Market Matrix. The remaining responses will fit into the SCOT Worksheet.

EMPLOYEE RESEARCH

Learning about client and prospect perceptions is an excellent way to get started on your research, but it is just as important to learn the perception of employees regarding your firm's strengths and challenges. In addition to learning critical information from them, you are also signaling to employees the value the firm places on their opinions and on their role as front-line marketers. You have the option of interviewing some or all employees individually or inviting them to come together as a group to participate in the SCOT analysis you are conducting. By asking employees to rate the firm's strengths, challenges, opportunities and threats you will quickly learn if your "experts" are on track in your areas of expertise and with your marketing goals.

A sample of interview questions for employee research:

"We are creating a strategic marketing plan for ABC Design for the coming year. Would you take a few minutes to answer questions that will assist the firm with the planning? Your responses will be confidential."

1. What do you see as ABC Design's strengths?
2. What do you see as ABC Design's challenges?
3. What do you see as ABC Design's threats?
4. What do you see as ABC Design's opportunities?

5. What do you think differentiates ABC Design from other firms?
6. What would you suggest ABC Design do to improve awareness in our vertical markets?

NOTE: The answers employees give to these questions fit into the SCOT Worksheet.

CONCLUSION

You have now completed a huge amount of work. Congratulations! You are sitting on a mountain of information; fortunately, it is sorted into two easy-to-comprehend worksheets. You have your finger on the pulse of what your market wants. Now, how to make sense of all that you have learned? By moving on to the next chapter, Assessment and Analysis.

ASSESSMENT AND ANALYSIS: WHERE ARE YOU NOW?

YOUR CURRENT STATUS

To effectively assess your current status, it is helpful to think of yourself as a tour guide who points to the past and says, "That is where we were," then looks around and says, "Here is where we are today," and, finally, looks to the horizon and says, "That is where we are going." Not only does this approach keep you grounded in the reality of today, but it helps to celebrate victories, to learn from mistakes in the past, and to remain inspired by the possibilities of tomorrow. Before you leave for tomorrow, however, a clear-eyed assessment of where you are today is in order.

At this point in formulating your marketing plan, major

research has been completed. Key questions have been asked and answered. You have heard from clients and know what they think of your firm, your work, and your employees, ranging from the level of design expertise to communication abilities to overall reputation. You have uncovered what clients, prospects, and employees think are your strengths and challenges as well as the various opportunities and threats that exist within your markets, and you have used the information to fill in the Vertical Market Worksheet and the SCOT Worksheet. Now it is time to review both of those worksheets. The former provides a picture of what you are doing in your vertical markets, while the latter provides a picture of your entire company. And, we are adding other assessment methods here: target market effectors, concentric circles, prospect ranking, the communication audit, and the publicity questionnaire.

ASSESSMENT: TARGET MARKET EFFECTORS—
AWARENESS, ATTITUDE, TRIAL, RETRIAL

We learned about target market effectors in *The Successful Marketing Plan: A Disciplined and Comprehensive Approach* by Roman G. Hiebing, Jr. and Scott W. Cooper. The authors state that target market effectors are awareness, attitude, trial, and retrial. In other words: Is your market aware of you, do they like you, have they contracted with you, and have they returned? Scoring your firm on these four points tells you just what you really want to know. For example, if people are favorable and have contracted with you more than once, then it is clear that your internal systems are working and that the key to growth is to simply build more awareness. Conversely, if you are doing a great job building awareness that results in a first contract but no repeat business, you need to look at and improve internal operations to build repeat business.

Scoring yourself on target market effectors can be as simple as interviewing colleagues in your firm and looking at your history with clients. Make a note of any strategies that come to you as a result of this assessment.

ASSESSMENT: CONCENTRIC CIRCLES

An easy and helpful way to think about marketing and growing your business is concentric circles. The inner circle represents where you operate today. The outer circles represent where you want to go. In order to grow, imagine, sticking your big toe out into the second concentric circle, all the while maintaining a hold on your inner circle as you develop the outer circle. Once the second circle is developed and both the first and second circles are solid, you can take the next step into the third circle. You can think about it geographically; for example, start in Boston, then move out to New England, then to the Northeast, or, you can think about it in terms of vertical markets. Either way, the concept of concentric circles will help you to assess where you are in your firm's growth. Make a note of any strategies that spring to mind as you do this assessment. You will want to hold on to them for further development in Chapter Eight.

CONCENTRIC CIRCLES

Concentric circles are an easy way to think about marketing. When you are assured that the relationships in your inner circle are cemented, you move into the next circle. Develop that circle, but hold onto the relationships in the inner circle. As you move outward, you have a wider degree of separation, but by managing your marketing, you will gain a foothold in each successive circle as you maintain a strong hold on the relationships established in the previous circles.

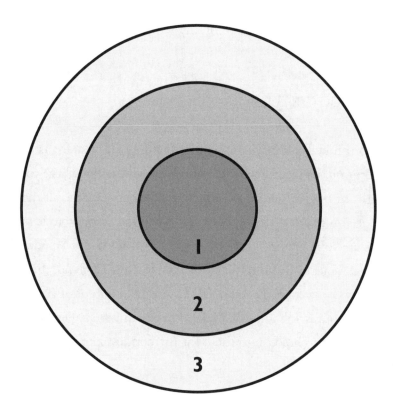

1. Inner circle: Your closest market, including your city, people you know, your current clients.
2. Second circle: Your second market including, your state, people you know less well, prospects.
3. Third circle: Your third market, including your region, prospects.

ASSESSMENT: RANKING PROSPECTS

In Chapter Eight, Strategies, you will read about creating mini-marketing plans targeted to one prospect with strategies that apply specifically to that prospect. We have seen design firms succeed with this idea, but to directly target a prospect in this way, you must rank the prospect. In the world of fundraising, it is not uncommon to rank prospective donors by "temperature." Stating how cold or warm prospective donors are at a certain point in the fundraising process is the clue as to how close they are to becoming a donor. Another way to do the same kind of ranking of prospects is to think in terms of courtship. By using the courtship continuum, we attempt to gauge where the relationship with a prospect stands and what the next strategy is for turning that prospect into a new client.

More specifically, if signing a contract can be seen as getting to the altar, then back up and see that to achieve that goal, you have to become engaged, and before that you have to go on several dates, and before that you have to ask someone out on a first date, and before that you have to meet the person, and before that you have to identify who that person is!

There are lessons to be learned from the courtship continuum. First, when we consult with clients, we often found it was not uncommon for prospects to be ranked farther along the spectrum than they actually were. Taking the time to rank them can be helpful in honestly assessing how close the prospect is to the altar. Second, although it seems obvious, it is helpful to remind ourselves that you can move a prospect from a long engagement to the altar more easily than you can get a prospect to the altar after just one date. And third, this metaphor reminds us that in our personal lives it takes a long time to literally get someone to the altar, and it is no different in the world of business. As with the concentric circle concept, you can either use the courtship continuum as a way to think about your marketing or you can take it a step further and actually rank each of your prospects and then use that information to create a mini-strategy for each one. Place all your prospects on the courtship continuum, evaluating each on their proximity to the altar. In Chapter Eight, Strategies, we will look at creating appropriate strategies to move them along by focusing first on those closest to the altar since there are fewer tasks associated with getting to "yes." If these processes sound corny, find your own way of ranking prospects so that you can create appropriate strategies to move them forward.

Courtship Continuum						
Prospects	Identify	Meet	First Date	Dating	Engaged	Altar

See: www.greenway.us/expertbook for this template

ASSESSMENT: AUDITING YOUR COMMUNICATIONS

We know that firms benefit from conducting an audit of their communications to locate gaps and overlap. We recommend looking at the four elements of communication—audience, message, vehicle, and frequency. These elements easily adapt to a worksheet format, and before you create a new campaign, we urge you to complete Communication Audit. In Chapter Eight, Strategies, we will revisit the Communication Audit and look at how to develop strategies from the audit. (Keep in mind that you are auditing what you are doing now. When you lay out your marketing plan, we recommend that you use this same form as a chart for your communication campaign.)

Fill in all the information that you know. Begin by listing your current audiences and the message you are sending to each one. Then fill in the vehicle you use and how often it is shared. Assessing what you are currently doing will give you a snapshot of your areas of success, areas that you are missing, and where you could use improvement. You may find that you have a key audience with a key message but that you have not found the right vehicle to get the word out. Success can be measured by assessing your communications and setting strategy to eliminate gaps and duplication. After we take you through the audit, we will show you how ABC Design filled in its audit.

Communication Audit				
Audience	Message	Vehicle	Frequency	Strategies

See: www.greenway.us/expertbook for this template

Audience: Your Staff

We feel that your first audience should always be your staff. Before moving on to clients, prospects, consultants, contractors, vendors, professional societies, the media, or the general public, your staff should be fully informed about the message and the communication vehicles you are using. Again, your employees are your front-line marketers. Everyone should be conveying the same message.

Audience: Your Clients, Your Prospects

For this worksheet, you can be as general as naming your vertical markets or as specific as naming the clients and prospects that you inserted into the Vertical Market Worksheet.

Audience: Influencers

Ask yourself who can influence targeted decision makers and list the titles or names in the Audience column in the worksheet. The information you have today may be quite general or very specific. For example, you may know that you want to reach the facilities manager at a certain large hospital or you may only have general thoughts, such as facilities managers of healthcare campuses across the state. As with each worksheet in this book, we recommend you list what you currently know and add further information as your knowledge expands.

Message

Again, you are auditing what you are currently communicating. Once your initial audit is complete, we recommend that you use this same form to chart out what you want to communicate in the future.

Vehicle

Many firms think in terms of advertising, press releases, brochures, and Web sites as the vehicles for their message, but you must look at every way in which you communicate or interact with clients and prospects, including invoicing, newsletters, e-mail, correspondence, speeches, seminars, and your trade show booth. Even more specifically, often when we think of advertising, we think of print advertising and can overlook the Internet, radio, and television as potential vehicles. Also view interoffice discussions and staff meetings as additional vehicles for delivering your positioning message and ensuring that everyone on staff is on the same page.

Frequency

We know from advertising industry studies that an advertisement has to be placed at least 10 times to get a message across. Given the plethora of vehicles at our disposal, we believe that the 10 times can include any type of communication that reaches your audience, whether an ad or e-mail, a speech or a story in the newspaper. Under Frequency on the worksheet, note the number of times you communicate with your audience, including the month or specific dates. For example, invoicing occurs monthly and seasonal outreach may occur four times a year, perhaps in the form of a print or digital newsletter.

When the audit is complete, you will see both the overlaps and the gaps in your efforts. When we get to Chapter Eight, we will focus on eliminating these by establishing a plan that capitalizes on the most appropriate opportunities for communicating to your selected audiences. You can make those notes in the last column: Strategy. Again, we will concentrate on strategies in Chapter Eight.

Communication Audit ABC Design				
Audience	Message	Vehicle	Frequency	Strategies
Staff	ABC Brand: Elevator speech Tag line	Staff Meetings	Weekly	Review/practice in staff meetings.
Clients				
1. Local hospital	We know high tech – update on trends, equipment, conferences attended.	E-news	Quarterly	
2. Eden retirement community	Master planning	Client and Local press	Monthly	Update client and public on planning process and progress
	Design underway	Client meetings	Monthly	Communicate ideas, showcase expertise
3. Ames secondary school	Master planning	Client and Local press	Monthly	Update client and public on planning process and progress
	Sustainable design	Client meetings	Monthly	Communicate ideas, showcase expertise
	Life-cycle cost analysis	Client meetings and Feature article		Communicate ideas, showcase expertise to client and in industry newsletter

Communication Audit ABC Design				
Audience	Message	Vehicle	Frequency	Strategies
Prospects				
1. County hospital	Renovation experts who can design new, improved services while maintaining essential services	Case History Prospect meeting	One mailing One time	Satisfied client Highlight scheduling, high tech expertise, problem solving
2. MRI clinic	Imaging department experts	Case History E-news Prospect meeting and portfolio	One mailing Quarterly One time	Satisfied client Update portfolio
3. Beacon Senior Living	Primary market, years of experience, team knowledge	Case History E-news Prospect meeting	One mailing Quarterly One time	Satisfied client Update portfolio

ASSESSMENT: MANAGING YOUR PUBLICITY - A QUESTIONNAIRE

This questionnaire is used in our seminars to help firms assess their publicity program. If you are able to answer yes to most of these questions, you are clearly on top of publicizing your firm; if you answer no to most of the questions, you have tasks to add to your To-Do List. Continue to make note of strategies that occur to you as you complete this questionnaire.

Publicity Questionnaire

1. Is there a person on staff assigned to publicity at your firm?

> Yes____ No____

2. Do you use outside publicity consultants?

> Yes____ No____

3. Does your system include a calendar that notes when content for a press release is triggered?
(For example: contract award, ground breaking, ribbon cutting, dedication, etc.)

> Yes____ No____

4. Have you identified your audiences for publicity?

> Yes____ No____

5. Are your publicity procedures written down?

> Yes____ No____

6. Have you targeted specific media outlets and reporters to pitch to?

> Yes____ No____

7. Is there a Communication Audit that shows where there might be duplication or gaps in publicity?

Yes____ No____

8. Have you created a media outlet database with, editors' and reporters' contact information, deadlines, and communication preferences (e-mail, postal service)?

Yes____ No____

9. Is the publicity person tracking these media outlets regularly to learn the interest of the publisher, editor or reporter?

Yes____ No____

10. Has the publicity person met face-to-face with the targeted writer/editor to create/build the relationship?

Yes____ No____

11. Is a clipping service being used?

Yes____ No____

12. If no, is the publicity person responsible for clipping?

Yes____ No____

13. Is a binder being kept of all clippings?

Yes____ No____

14. Is there a standard media kit?

Yes____ No____

15. Is there an Articles Archive?

Yes____ No____

16. Are articles sent routinely to your audiences?

       Yes____ No____

17. Is development of story ideas a regular task for the publicity person?

       Yes____ No____

18. Is there a Story Idea Archive?

       Yes____ No____

19. Is there an Image Archive?

       Yes____ No____

CONCLUSION

You have used several methods to assess where you are as a firm with your prospects and in your internal management functions. Sometimes we err on the side of seeing only what is positive and are blinded to the negative; sometimes it is exactly the opposite. There is nothing better than being clear about both. With that thought in mind, we now move on to how you are going to take all you have learned and create the positioning message for your firm.

POSITIONING YOUR FIRM AND YOUR DESIGNERS: HOW DO YOU CREATE THE MESSAGE?

THE POSITIONING MESSAGE

In this chapter we look at how to craft the positioning message about your firm and your designers.

Imagine, once again, that conversation in which a prospect asks someone in the community for the name of the person who can design the state-of-the-art hospital facility and the instant response is the name of one of your associates. We stated that the response is the result of your efforts to disseminate critical information about your firm knowledge and your employees as experts to your vertical market. When the person—your Vertical Market Leader—who heads up that initiative is named, you have achieved both successful personal branding and successful firm positioning.

Positioning refers to the perception your market has of you: literally, the position your firm holds in the mind of the consumer. To achieve positioning, you need to create a message for your market that combines two ideas: what you are selling—the knowledge and expertise you have "on the shelf," and your clients' needs. This message must powerfully state how you can meet those needs more effectively than the competition. In the case of your employee being named as the go-to expert, that is the result of communicating the message in your market that you know what your clients and prospects want and that you have the expert who can meet their needs.

In the research process, we mentioned that it is not unusual to learn that what *you* think is not what *other'* think. For example, what you may assess as your firm's greatest strength may not be what your clients think of as your greatest strength. Since it is critical to the whole marketing process to understand who you are and how you are perceived, you will want to take client perceptions fully into account as you create your positioning message because, again, the bottom line is "Business comes to the expert." By combining client perception and client needs with your knowledge, you will be able to differentiate yourself from your competition. You will have your positioning message.

We see over and over again that clients need the assurance that the designers who are servicing their projects know what needs to be done and have the expertise to not only design but to lead a team and produce the desired result. Once clients and prospects are convinced that designers know their subject, they want to discuss it in plain, convincing language. So be assured that clients and prospects do read articles and columns written by you, the expert; attend seminars and conferences led by you, the expert; and will come up to talk to you, the expert, when the opportunity arises.

You know your own story and you can tell it better than anyone. By adding knowledge about client and prospect challenges to your story, you are signaling to them that you understand their project needs and challenges. The positioning message is your opening to blow your own horn. You must do just that so clients will know you are a capable team with the depth of knowledge and expertise they need.

Create your positioning message by reviewing all the sources of information that feed into it: your Book of Knowledge, your mission statement, your case histories, and your research findings. Then distill the information to create your specific positioning message and use it in various vehicles to demonstrate that you know what your clients and prospects want and that you can provide solutions that will meet their needs and enhance their projects. Remember that the structure of your positioning message, regardless of the words you ultimately choose, must be "I know what you want and I've got it."

The report you have compiled from your internal and external research surveys (research questions to employees, clients, and prospects) cites essential information about the firm's strengths, which you will incorporate into your positioning statement and marketing materials. You know your strengths, you know how the team rises to challenges, and you have specific comments (in the form of testimonials) from clients regarding firm resources. All this information, once condensed, easily transfers to use in firm brochures, press releases, informative e-mails, and other vehicles.

DISTILLING THE MESSAGE

As we said before, the world may not be interested in your entire Book of Knowledge. You want to distill it into smaller bits of information that will be of most interest to your audience, including your mission statement, case histories, story ideas, your elevator speech, and your tagline.

The best place to start is with case histories—those one sheet, at-a-glance summaries of your projects. They are a great way to translate your knowledge into meaningful communications for the market since they contain the following three elements: the challenge presented by the client, the recommendation presented by your firm, and the result (client testimonial). Once you have completed your case histories, you have a great source of story ideas for the media, for seminars, columns, press releases, newsletters, and your Web site. All of the knowledge about your firm can be further condensed into your mission statement, your elevator speech, and your tagline.

Here is how ABC Design telescoped its knowledge and mission statement into an elevator speech and, finally, into a tagline. As we mentioned in Chapter One, ABC Design is an urban firm, serving two primary markets, senior living and healthcare, and a secondary market in education. With specialties in historic preservation and sustainability that crossed over all three markets, they named their book of knowledge *Sustainable Restoration Solutions*.

Mission Statement: ABC Design is committed to infrastructure design and historic renovation that enhances communities in senior living, healthcare, and education. We are further committed to maintaining a knowledgeable staff that can provide sustainable, accessible, and cost-effective designs that are user-friendly.

Elevator Speech: ABC Design provides designs to communities that need up-to-date, cost-effective senior living, healthcare, and educational spaces. We are a group of dedicated problem solvers who focus on providing new buildings and historic preservation that look good, save money, save the environment and serve their users well.

Tagline: Sustainable restoration solutions … and more!

THE MISSION STATEMENT

We begin with the key element of your positioning message, the mission statement, which is a brief description of a company's fundamental purpose and answers the question "Why do we exist?" In addition, your statement, sometimes referred to as your philosophy or manifesto, is a way to describe your unique outlook and inform all your communication. The mission statement articulates the company's purpose both for those in the organization and for the public. It is generally 100 words or less and is crafted by the firm leaders and brainstormed among the entire staff or, if more feasible, developed with a selected focus group. Developing a mission statement is evidence of commitment to a purpose and is an important part of the process of distilling your message from the broad arena of "why do we exist," to the more condensed message of an elevator speech, to the final, compressed slogan known as a tagline.

THE ELEVATOR SPEECH

The mission statement can be distilled down to the elevator speech, a slang term for a marketing technique in which you have approximately 30 seconds to inform or persuade someone about your product or service. It is so named because it can be delivered in the time span of an elevator ride. It includes mention of your product or service, the associated features and benefits, and a call to action. By refining the core message in your mission statement and practicing the delivery, it is possible to convey a solid positioning message in just half a minute.

This message is the one you will convey in every face-to-face meeting and is the one that will travel by word of mouth throughout your audiences. Developing your elevator speech is a creative process that may take several weeks to refine, but the result is worth the effort as it once again tells your audiences, "I know what you want, and I've got it!"

THE TAGLINE

The elevator speech can be further distilled into your tagline. The term refers to a brief, evocative slogan or phrase that conveys the most important attribute or benefit of your company, product, or service that the advertiser wishes to convey. A tagline is generally a theme to a campaign and we are familiar with myriad taglines. For example, Dell Computer's tagline is "Easy as Dell;" Verizon's is "We Never Stop Working for You;" and Newman's Own is "Shameless Exploitation in Pursuit of the Common Good." (All taglines in our examples are the trademarks or service marks of their respective owners.) Your 10 words or less will represent the essence of your positioning.

To get started on crafting a tagline, we urge our students and seminar participants to look at the underlying structure of well-known taglines. Upon pondering the old General Electric tagline, "Where progress is our most important product," we see the structure "where x is y." One nonprofit selling top-quality crafts used that formula to create the tagline "Where excellence is handcrafted." A design firm might use "Where design challenges are satisfied." You may choose to never use a tagline, but we urge you to complete the process because it forces you to condense your positioning message to the fewest, most powerful words.

THE CASE HISTORY

Now that we have looked at your institutional firm-wide messaging, we will take another look at your project-related knowledge to see how that specific knowledge can be distilled into powerful messages. Case histories are one of the most important ways to translate your knowledge into meaningful communications for your markets. Case histories are also referred to as case studies, project histories, project synopses, or project closeout reports, but regardless of the title, they are an encapsulation of the critical elements of a project.

Case histories pack the most punch when they reflect your expertise, include a client testimonial, are contained on a single page, and feature a dynamic photograph. They will best convey your critical message when structured to answer these three questions:

- What was the challenge presented by the client?

- What was the recommendation of our firm?

- What was the result? (The client testimonial is featured here.)

Client testimonials present an opportunity to differentiate yourself from your competition. The contract negotiation period is a good time to discuss testimonials and to agree on written feedback between designer and client. Testimonials can spring from client and prospect interviews or from the normal course of business, and obtaining them is critical since a third-party endorsement is always the best verification of abilities. Affirmation from a satisfied client that "ABC Design is the greatest thing since sliced bread" is always better than proclaiming on your own behalf, "My firm is the greatest thing since sliced bread."

Make it a requirement and an ongoing task for Vertical Market Leaders to create a case history that includes a testimonial and great photographs for every major project to be properly archived in your Book of Knowledge. Throughout the year, the marketing team should review case histories and select topics as story ideas to feature in all vehicles, including speeches, press releases, direct mail, Web site and articles, and mandate that all communication vehicles be reviewed frequently to be sure that they contain the most up-to-date information.

ABC DESIGN CASE HISTORY

The Project: 60-Unit Senior Living Project

ABC teamed with a regional non-profit Senior Living developer to design and construct a sustainable, 60-unit Senior Living community on metropolitan acreage. The result is a three-story, 200,000-square-foot residential complex for seniors who wish to give up their city homes but not their city lifestyle. The unit mix includes 20 studio apartments, 35 one-bedroom, and five two-bedroom apartments. The building is completely accessible and features two elevator banks that conveniently transport residents from the underground parking to each level.

Residents have a range of services available, including laundry, housekeeping, and common meals, and medical staff is available to provide assistance with medications and other activities of daily living as needed. The common areas located on each level are designed to promote a neighborhood environment and accommodate a variety of group activities.

The Challenge: Incorporate sustainable, cost-saving design while providing a homey atmosphere for senior residents.

The Recommendation: Use sustainable, easy-care finishes throughout, from common areas to specialty areas to apartments. Promote the homey, neighborhood atmosphere by providing multi-use, community space on each living level; ground floor outdoor space with pathways, seating, and gardening opportunities; and garage space for both private and community vehicles.

The Result: A satisfied client and happy residents.

Testimonial: Client comments, "ABC Design had the expertise and experience to easily accommodate our request for a sustainable design and thrilled us with the level of community they skillfully incorporated in their overall design."

Testimonial: Resident states, "I am completely at ease with my transition to this new apartment. My neighbors and I couldn't be happier with our decision to come here."

STORY IDEAS

Each case history can be distilled into story ideas, a term used in publicity to describe the brief pitch or the angle used to interest a reporter in a story. You can use a story idea to pitch your in-house expert as a panelist or lecturer for a conference or as a writer for a column in an industry newsletter. We use it here to emphasize condensing what you have to say to a client or prospect into a few convincing words. Your story ideas can come from a variety of sources, especially from case histories where you matched a client need with your firm knowledge to recommend and create a solution. This tying together of information is how you position your firm as the go-to experts.

One of the best examples of story ideas for a design firm is when you are able to talk about how your firm is on the cutting edge of a national trend. This allows a reporter to cover what is both a national story and a local story. Here is a successful example from the world of music meeting the world of design. In the article "Making Music Today/State-of-the-Art Home Recording Studio", according to *Billboard's* Christopher Walsh, "The proliferation of ever-improving digital audio workstations (DAW) into more and more home studios" is partly responsible for the contracting and consolidating of the music business. In the same 2002 article, John Storyk of the Walters-Storyk Design Group that designs home studios, says, "We're continuing to see what I call 'desktop audio'…. It's in a composer's home, but it's a full-on professional studio. This is the typical studio of the 21st century." BRR Records has become a part of that movement by recording its artists on high-end equipment at home in the country. According to one musician/producer/recording engineer, "These changes have allowed us to move toward doing it ourselves, to staying closer to home in the comfort zone, and to working when we want to work. I think it brings a more relaxed quality to our music."

Another example of a story idea is to take a commonly held perception and turn it on its head. For example, we found success in pitching the media a story about a green renovation with the lead in "All green buildings are new, right? Not necessarily. Take a look at this recently renovated and restored municipal building—a public showcase of renewable energy technologies."

Finally, another story idea is to divulge a secret. Here is another successful pitch where the secret was part of an e-mail blitz: "TR Group discovers the secret to successful green architecture. Lesson learned after just cutting the ribbon on its new green regional headquarters? 'You can't do green alone.' So says the chair of the board of directors of the TR Group. 'It was a great collaboration between donor, client and designers. You can't point to any one thing and say it was the result of a specific person. It was the team.'"

INSTRUCTIONS FOR CREATING YOUR POSITIONING MESSAGE

Your goal is to create an accurate and effective positioning message by reviewing what you know and then applying that wealth of information to the various communication vehicles you will share with your public. Review your Book of Knowledge and all the research results that you charted in both the Vertical

Market Worksheet and the SCOT Worksheet regarding client, prospect, and employee perception of your firm. Search the results for exactly what clients and prospects stated as their design needs and what they want from a designer. Look at your current positioning information to gauge if you are on message or if you need to update your message. If you feel you are not on message, brainstorm with staff to create the unique, clear, and powerful message that states what you are selling and how your service or product serves your clients' design needs. Then condense the message into an elevator speech and even further into a tagline.

STORING ALL YOUR MARKETING CONTENT

- **Create a boilerplate content folder.** Save all of this content—positioning message, mission statement, elevator speech, tagline, etc.—as boilerplate copy for easy retrieval and use in all your marketing materials, including your Web site, print and electronic brochures, e-news, newsletters, etc.

- **Create a Story Idea Archive.** Review your knowledge and distill story ideas from case histories, personnel profiles, corporate events, and national trends that your firm is part of or a new research report of interest to your clients and prospects. The Story Idea Archive will complement your Image Archive of wonderful photographs. Add to it on a regular basis. Keep it categorized for easy retrieval for press releases, speeches, media pitches and client presentations.

- **Create an Image Archive.** File your high-resolution photographs so they can be easily e-mailed or downloaded from a media room on your Web site. Include employee head shots for Web and press releases.

- **Create an archive of press releases, columns, and articles.** Catalogue all releases. When one of your employee experts writes a column or when a reporter writes an article, be sure to archive these pieces. They will be invaluable for future marketing with clients, prospects, and influencers.

- **Include press releases, columns, and articles on your Web site.** Place this information in chronological order and make it available to the public.

DISSEMINATING THE MESSAGE

Now you are ready to disseminate the knowledge to your vertical markets through speaking and writing opportunities. In Chapter Seven, Tools, we will fully discuss how your designated employees will be positioned as the experts, the go-to people on particular topics with the goal that when clients and prospects need expertise, your firm and the experts within will come to mind first. Once the message is created, you can:

- Disseminate the message to all employees and reinforce their importance as marketers.

- Revisit the message during regular staff meetings to reinforce with employees "who we are, what we provide, and where we are going."

- Use the message in all interactions with clients, prospects, vendors, and the general public.

- Use the message and highlight case histories on all materials for client, prospect, and public.

- Cite your expertise and knowledge in all vehicles to highlight your design abilities as well as your analytical skills and technical knowledge.

- Review your message on a regular basis to confirm that you remain on message as new knowledge comes into the firm.

ARE YOU WELL POSITIONED?

As the Oracle at Delphi said, "Know thyself." It applies to you as well. You are well positioned if you:

- Know your markets
- Know your prospects

- Know what they want

- Know your strengths and challenges

- Market your individual designers as the go-to experts.

- Define your firm's expertise

- Conduct research to learn if your name is recognized and recommended.

CONCLUSION

You have now successfully determined how best to position your firm and your designers in the marketplace. You have confirmed your mission statement, crafted your positioning statement, pulled together case histories, created story ideas, and condensed all of this into the bite-size pieces that will intrigue your market. Now we are ready to look at the big picture and lay out the goals that will transform your firm. On to Chapter Six!

GOALS: WHERE DO YOU WANT TO GO?

MOVING FORWARD

Setting goals is essential. Whether you are a newly established firm or have been in business for several years, you want to move forward in a logical and productive manner with your eye on designated targets. By definition, a goal is that which you are aiming for: Become a regional leader in the higher education market or increase revenue by 10% in higher education in one year, form example. Strategies are the means to the goal: network with influencers, get testimonials from past clients, and improve communication with school leaders. We recommend that you spell out your goals in both narrative and financial terms.

Part of the process of managing your marketing is to understand how goals are set and who is setting them. The owner and principals in a firm have the major input regarding goals because they accepted the responsibility of establishing and growing their design practice. They will rely heavily on their marketing and accounting staff for statistical input and upon the entire staff for support and suggestions, and they will take all the past year's activities into consideration, but it generally falls upon these leaders to ultimately determine the goals for each year.

Goals come from a variety of sources: from determining your strengths and what you enjoy accomplishing as a team; from perceptions of your firm by clients and prospects; from ambitions to be more profitable, larger, and more well-known; and from your current assessment of the firm. The key to moving forward is to set specific, positive, and achievable goals. If you set a goal that, upon further consideration, seems beyond your reach, break it down to smaller, more achievable segments. Be sure that your goals are also achievable within your timeframe, your financial means, and the current expertise of your staff.

When consulting, we ask our clients to participate in a standard visioning exercise. Try it now. Envision receiving an achievement award at some point in the future, say, in two years. Imagine you are at an awards banquet and your name has been called from the stage. As you approach the podium, you are handed a certificate. You open it and read it. What does it say? If you can imagine what it says and the achievement you are being recognized for, you have established a goal.

List that goal and any others that you have set, in the Goals Worksheet. In past chapters, you may have made note of several strategies you would like to use, from the Vertical Market Worksheet and SCOT

Worksheet in Chapter Three, or any of the assessment methods in Chapter Four. As you write down the goals below, strategies may occur to you immediately, so note them as well. We will remind you as we move into Chapter Seven that *all* strategies, no matter their source, must be linked to a goal or they should not be included in your plan. Once you have listed all your goals and all the corresponding strategies, you will list the tactics that will bring your goals to fruition. Those tactics will be listed on the final To-Do List which will drive your marketing efforts. The worksheet below is a good document to refer to regularly to see how you are progressing on the path to achievement.

Goals Worksheet		
Goal	Strategy	Tactic

See: www.greenway.us/expertbook for this template

DESCRIBING YOUR GOALS IN NARRATIVE FORM

Stating your vision for the future in a narrative form may be somewhat of a challenge, but it's a challenge that we encourage you to accept. (And when we use the word narrative we mean the qualitative goals as contrasted to the quantitative or financial goals you are setting. The "narrative" can be as simple as listing them in the Goals Worksheet.) Document your goals as a part of your marketing plan to avoid confusion and to send the message to staff that firm leaders are serious about determining and achieving goals. Writing a narrative provides a clear picture of where you want to be at the end of a specific period of time, whether months or years. Beyond just listing the goals in the worksheet, you can go further and describe how the goal relates to the services you currently provide or want to provide in the future (your knowledge), the way you provide services (your expertise), and the employees with the expertise (celebrities). Goal setting should be made in the context of your current markets and industry forecasts, which will provide you direction and promote reasonable expectations.

Focusing on goals and writing the narrative is one part of the annual plan that provides the big picture for the year ahead. This is a document that the entire staff can read to understand where the firm is headed and why. Here is the outline for ABC Design's narrative.

ABC Design has set the following goals.

In five years:

- To be branded and compete nationally in senior living and healthcare.

- To secure high profile breakthrough projects with ample budgets.

- To take our successful regional firm, strengthen it, and launch it as a national firm.

In two years:

- Recruit the best talent and work on challenging projects for clients who value design.

- Provide top quality client service.

- Create award-winning design that can be published.

- Plan for upturn in senior living vertical market.

- Offer clients expertise in the latest technology.
- Build sustainability into firm culture.

In one year:

- Implement the strategic marketing plan.
- Increase revenue in the strongest vertical market (senior living) by 10%.
- Expand geographic territory and secure first major senior living project in new geographic area.
- Personally brand our vertical market leaders in senior living and healthcare; find a leader for education market.
- Continue responding to Requests for Proposals while increasing our proactive marketing.

Quantitative goals:

- Increase senior living vertical market revenue by 10% a year for three years.
- Increase healthcare vertical market revenue by 10% a year for three years.
- Increase education vertical market revenue by 5% a year for three years.

In addition to ABC Design's goals, here are others we hear from our clients that may coincide with the goals that you have set or provide inspiration for future goals.

- Get x% or $x more work from current clients.
- Continue to satisfy clients.
- Be more proactive in finding new work.
- Convince clients to award us more complex projects.
- Break into a new market where we have peripheral experience.
- Increase revenue by x%.
- More clearly define who we are.
- Change our revenue mix to a higher percentage from x market.
- Broaden our vertical markets.
- Narrow our vertical markets.
- Move into new geographic territory.
- Gain more confidence in networking and selling the accomplishments of the firm.
- Make time to market.
- Get to a point of no cold calling, just warm calls.
- Sell our strengths.
- Uncover opportunities.
- Make time for proactive business development while still responding to Requests for Proposals.
- Stay focused on stability, profitability, and growth.
- Promote personal growth and professional development.
- Be recognized by our peers.

FINANCIAL GOALS

Every firm must set annual revenue goals. Normally, the annual budget (see Chapter 11, Budget, for more information) is based on the expectation of reaching financial benchmarks, so the motivation for success is compelling. You can set your financial goals in a variety of ways:

- Make a firm-wide projection based on previous growth.

- Look at each vertical market and make a projection based on both your firm's history of growth in that market and the industry's projections for growth in that market.

- Look at current and projected project fees and add a percentage for growth.

- Use a combination of these methods, as they test each other.

It is important to keep good statistical records to help you make good financial decisions. You will want to know the percentages of your current mix of work, the percentage of income from each market, and the percentage of change in income per market per year. In addition, track the change, up or down, in the number of employees and projects you handle from year to year so you can determine the relationship between project volume (in gross fees) and the number of people it takes to produce that volume.

Review how your firm has been performing in your vertical markets, how those markets are growing, and how many new resources you can bring to bear on a targeted market. If you are considering venturing into a new market, take into account how much effort you intend to put into that goal, remembering that the marketing-to-sales ratio guideline is to add 2% to 3% of gross revenue to the marketing budget if collateral materials are being redone or if you are entering a new market. This expense is over and above what you are already spending on marketing, the standard marketing budget being 5% to 15% of gross revenues. The budgets on the higher side generally include salaries allocated to marketing.

When all is said and done, our big-picture goal is simply that our audiences know, value, and pay for what we offer. Sounds simple, but there is work to accomplish to get to that point! Before you proceed to the next chapters, write on the worksheet the goals that have come to mind as you have considered incorporating knowledge management as the means to improving your client base and overall success.

CONSIDER THIS…
Where are you headed?
Who do you want for clients?
What do your clients want or need?
Who has the money?
What new trends can be taken advantage of with your current knowledge and expertise?

CONCLUSION

You have now laid out goals for your firm in both words and numbers. You may already be realizing that you have too many to accomplish. If so, you can either trim back the number of goals or extend the time line for completing the goals. Also you may realize that you have more strategies listed from previous chapters than you have goals to link with the strategies. So you may need to add additional goals or delete some of the strategies. Before we get to the specifics of strategies, we will consider the tools you will use to make your dreams come true.

TOOLS: HOW BEST TO DELIVER YOUR MESSAGE?

7

WARMING UP YOUR AUDIENCE

Before we get to specific strategies in the next chapter, we want to stop and look at all the tools you have at your disposal to build awareness of both your firm's and your employees' expertise in your markets and to manage the administrative duties in your marketing department. We will cover how to use professional societies to build awareness of your experts, how to look at your trigger points for communications throughout the year (groundbreaking, ribbon cutting, etc.), how to draw on your Story Idea Archive and how to refine your marketing machine so it works smoothly for you.

You may recall a study done some years back that found that an advertisement had to be placed at least 10 times to get a message across. Given the plethora of vehicles available to you today, we believe that these 10 times can include *any* type of communication that reaches your audience, whether it is an advertisement or an e-mail, a speech or a story in the newspaper. By using a variety of vehicles, you hope that when your targeted prospect receives a direct mail from you, the response will be, "Didn't I just hear her speak at last month's seminar?" Or "Didn't I just read a column by him in our industry newsletter?" The key here is to ensure that there are no cold calls because you have warmed up your audience.

YOUR VISUAL IDENTITY: GRAPHIC DESIGN AND PHOTOGRAPHY

You have developed the general positioning message for your firm and have refined it to suit your vertical markets. Now for the other half of the equation: matching the words with great visuals. Your visual identity is a tool that supports your key messages across a spectrum of communication vehicles. Since visual images are so critical to the design industry, the management of your graphics is the starting point for all that is to come in the various vehicles that will deliver your message to the public. You do not want to underestimate the importance of having a graphic designer and photographer either on staff or under contract for a dedicated number of hours per month. Find the people who can accurately represent your firm in visual form. Graphic design starts with the treatment of the company name on such items as the business card and letterhead and tracks all the way through your presentation materials, capabilities brochure, Web site, e-mails and every other piece of promotional material. Powerful photography is essential to showcase your design abilities and to bring your design solutions to the attention of your audience. Maintaining a specific look throughout all materials is critical because you want to present a consistent graphic image that aligns with your consistent written message.

THE To-Do List FOR GRAPHIC DESIGN AND PHOTOGRAPHY

- Calculate the cost of salaried positions or freelance contracts for graphic designer and photographer.

- Review portfolios for graphic designer and photographer.

- Hire or contract graphic designer and photographer.

- Take inventory and evaluate current marketing materials (see checklist that follows).

- If a new look is warranted, work with graphic designer to modify materials.

- Create schedule for modifying all marketing materials.

- Set and document graphic design standards for all promotional materials, paying particular attention to choices for logo, typeface, colors, use of tagline, and writing style.

- Create shot list of needed photography.

THE CAPABILITIES BROCHURE AND YOUR WEB SITE

While your brochure may be print, digital, or both, this is the central piece for all your communications. Because it describes and demonstrates who you are and what your capabilities are, it is often called the capabilities brochure. With your positioning message as the centerpiece, it can include your mission statement, case histories with testimonials, information about your team, the benefits of working with your firm, and of course, great photography.

DIGITAL COMMUNICATIONS

When a prospective client searches the Internet for design expertise within your vertical market, does your firm's name come up on the screen? To help prospects find you, include pertinent information about your practice on your Web site that contains key words associated with projects and solutions, employees and community involvement, columns and speeches employees have authored, and articles written about your firm. We are not suggesting that you overwhelm the reader with information, but we do suggest that you tease readers with brief information on the home page and include a "read more" link that will take them to another page with full information.

Depending on the size of your firm, you may have a technology guru in-house who develops and updates your Web site, or you may use a consulting firm to design your Web site and assign the responsibility for updates to your Marketing Coordinator. The key to a praiseworthy Web site is keep it user-friendly and loaded with up-to-date information.

In your research, you learned how prospects and clients want you to communicate with them. If their interest is in receiving news via e-mail, you want to be prepared with an e-news system that will allow you to insert content into an e-news format, merge it with a database of client and prospect e-mail addresses, and send it out. As with all other communications, be clearly focused on the benefit to readers, be brief, but with a "read more" link that will take them to the Web site for additional information.

To administer the e-news system effectively, follow up on all messages that bounce back to maintain a clean e-mail database. Review reports that show how many people in your audience received the e-news, how many opened it, how many clicked through, and exactly what content they reviewed. You then have valuable information to support continual improvement of your e-news. You can obtain e-mail addresses in a variety of ways, including having an e-news signup on your Web site, using your professional society and industry organizations that share member e-mails, and through personal contact.

ADVERTISING

Before you begin any advertising campaign, review your research and remind yourself of what your audience is paying attention to—what are they listening to, reading, and watching. Depending on the vehicles they have cited, you have several options for creating a campaign. First, consider the three types of media—trade, business, and consumer—and choose to use one, two, or all three. Within those three categories are newspaper and magazine, radio, television, and Internet. Some of these media outlets are commercial, others nonprofit. The goal is to advertise in the media that gets your message into the hands of your clients and prospects in order to sell your firm and notify them that you have the expertise they are seeking. Your decision as to which media to use and how often will be based on your research, your vertical markets, and your budget. In working with a media outlet, establish a relationship with an account representative who can help you put across the most effective message to your audience.

In addition to media outlets, there are many nonprofit organizations associated with various vertical markets as well as community events that welcome advertising throughout the year. Rates run the gamut of affordability and present varying options for short- or long-term campaigns. Again, you want to base your decision about which outlets to use on your understanding of which will gain the attention of your clients and prospects.

You may have a sense of the amount of advertising you can afford to include in your marketing budget, but if you are unfamiliar or unsure, we find that firms spend between 5% and 15% of gross revenues on marketing, and a part of that total marketing budget is apportioned to advertising. Look for more information in Chapter 11, Budget.

During the startup period, some firms may feel that paying for advertising is simply out of reach. We discuss bootstrapping, piggybacking, and bartering in the budget chapter, but for now, you can determine where you would place ads if you had the funds and include the line item in your marketing budget as a no go for this year. When you revisit advertising for next year's budget, you can lock in an affordable advertising campaign. In the meantime, be sure to include those targeted media outlets (present and future) in your database and regularly send press releases to them to attempt to land a mention or an article.

One of the most powerful forms of advertising, and the one that is free, is word of mouth. Thinking back to the startup phase when you broadcast the fact that you were in business to everyone who would listen, you can recall the power of word of mouth. It is important that all employees understand their role in absorbing and carrying the positioning message throughout their personal and professional networks. Face-to-face meetings between employees and clients, prospects and influencers can occur multiple times per day and every encounter is an opportunity to demonstrate your expertise.

PUBLICITY

The difference between advertising and publicity is that in advertising you select and pay for vehicles in which you can promote your expertise; in publicity you attempt to obtain media coverage by providing media outlets with information about your expertise and upcoming events. People often think of publicity as free, but it takes time and effort to make publicity work for you, and there is no guarantee of coverage.

One key to success with publicity is to name the person responsible. Just as we have encouraged you to name a Knowledge Leader and Vertical Market Leaders, we encourage you to confirm the importance of publicity as a management function by assigning the task to someone as the in-house single contact point. That employee will be proactive in turning story ideas into press releases, maintaining relationships with reporters and editors, attempting to keep your firm in the news, and responding to reporters' questions regarding design expertise, projects, or other activities of the firm.

Another key to success is to look at publicity from a reporter's perspective. Media outlets often have a requirement of a minimum number of stories that a reporter files each day. Think of what that means to reporters. They must find a story idea, pitch the angle to an editor and get approval, do the research, find people for interviews, interview them, send out a photographer, write the story, send it to the editor, get it back for rewrite, and finally, it becomes news. Imagine doing that for several stories a day and you can see that many reporters appreciate help with story ideas. In short, they need the content you possess.

Pay attention to which reporters are writing about your area of expertise, and start building a relationship by sending a note of appreciation for a well-written article. Being a fan of reporters is important as they are under-appreciated artists. Further, provide reporters with story ideas and recommendations of people for the reporter to interview, and offer to provide background research. Add reporters and editors to your database under media outlets and proactively communicate with the outlets in your community and in your vertical markets by sending press releases and story ideas. Be aware of *all* news outlets that could help you reach your target markets. Include your local resources, but also explore business media outlets such as the Chamber of Commerce and trade outlets such as industry magazines and newsletters. Finally, look at your Story Idea Archive and construct your press release schedule for the year. What are your trigger points for releases: contract award, groundbreaking, ribbon cutting, new expertise or award presentation?

PUBLICITY MEDIA KITS

Creating the media kit and sending out press releases is an ongoing publicity task. The media kit is a collection of information you send to the media that includes a story idea (also referred to as the pitch or the angle) that you hope reporters and editors will find intriguing, along with a press release with company information, suggestions for people to interview, and a fact sheet that provides background information on the story. It also includes appropriate images, copyrights, captions, and credits. Using the premise of needing to expose your name 10 times for it to become familiar to the public, many design firms send out monthly press releases.

Be proactive and remain prepared for the three key situations that require a media kit: routine media requests, a crisis, and the intriguing story idea you want to pitch. Some firms have a Media Room on their Web sites where the media kit and additional project information and images can be reviewed and downloaded by the reporter.

Sending a media kit is only the first step. It is helpful to remember that the ball is still in your court and follow-up is vital. After you send a kit, contact the reporter or editor to confirm that it was received and whether the information was of interest. It is not uncommon to be told that your release was not received. If that is the case, double check your contact information and resend, and be sure the correct contact information finds its way to your database. It is often a challenge to connect with media personnel so be persistent in your efforts to follow up on press releases. If you are informed that there is further interest in a topic or a building, arrange a personal interview or a tour. If you are informed that there is no interest, ask what topics would be of interest and make a note of that information for the future. Keep in mind that opportunities may arise—something happens on the national scene and local reporters may be interested to know that you have on staff an expert who can speak to that issue. You can let them know this by issuing that information as a media advisory. That information may benefit you down the road when the media again is looking for an expert on a similar topic.

Before you arrange to have any one of your experts interviewed by the media, consider coaching them on how best to handle the interview. Tips like staying on topic, not speculating, and speaking in clear, everyday language will improve the interview. If your firm and its experts are popular with the media, it would be worthwhile to have a media consultant provide an in-house workshop once a year.

The final part of the process is tracking and disseminating the coverage you receive. Learn when your article or interview will appear or will be broadcast. When it appears in print, get reprint permissions and make copies for the appropriate audiences, send the link to your audience via broadcast e-mail and include it on your Web site. You can record and link a video, as well, and all can be deposited into your Articles Archive on your Web site. The media kit is a significant investment of knowledge, time, and money so you need to know what return you are getting on your effort. Ask people in your market areas if they saw an article or a broadcast and ask for feedback as you want to use media coverage to its best effect.

USING PROFESSIONAL SOCIETIES: JOINING, SPEAKING, AND WRITING

We can not stress enough the importance of involvement with professional societies since they provide a great opportunity for delivering your knowledge message. Take advantage of this by becoming an active participant in regional and national activities of societies that represent your markets. These include organizations like the American Seniors Housing Association, the American Healthcare Association, and the National Association of Independent Schools. Research the societies within your vertical markets and decide which ones will be the best venues for participation by your Vertical Market Leaders and other designated employees. Before you become a member and send off your dues, read their publications and attend your first meeting as a guest.

Inquire about opportunities for involvement such as serving on a committee, speaking on a panel or in a seminar, or writing a column or article for the association's newsletter. Remembering that business comes to the expert, pitch your firm's Vertical Market Leaders as speakers and writers on the topics suggested by your Book of Knowledge. Be prepared with resumes or biographies and a list of speaker topics to use when recommending your firm's experts.

In addition to the opportunities mentioned above to disseminate your firm's knowledge, you may want to consider budgeting time, people and money to exhibit at shows and conferences related to your markets. The goal is for your Vertical Market Leader to be seen by the professional society members and other attendees as the expert to contact on particular projects. When attending professional meetings, trade shows or conferences, load up on and distribute business cards and follow up with people you meet as soon as possible upon your return to the office.

Take the time to find the decision makers and the influencers in your vertical markets. Once you have identified a vertical market, you have to drill down deep to identify specific individual decision makers and those who influence them. Membership in a professional society is a good way to learn who makes the final decisions regarding design projects. At colleges and universities it could be the head of facilities, head of buildings and grounds, or the campus planner, for example. When appropriate, contact decision makers directly or if you know influencers—alumni, members of the board of trustees, employees—contact these people and let them carry your message to the decision makers for you. Remember to add these contacts to your marketing database and to contact them on a regular basis.

NETWORKING

To complete the loop on setting goals and strategies, designers must be positioned to hear as much as they tell. In other words, word of potential projects should make its way to the firm as soon as possible. The best way to achieve this goal is to be positioned in a valuable networking community of influential contacts and decision makers, including property owners, developers, bankers, lawyers, accountants, real estate brokers, builders, community leaders and spokespeople, other design professionals, vendors, suppliers, and past and current clients. Participation in local, structured networking forums and maintenance of informal networking groups is valuable, as is active participation in professional and community-based organizations.

Get others—developers, builders, engineers, and vendors—to be your ambassadors by providing them with your firm's capabilities brochures. Revisit these industry leaders on a regular basis to keep them updated on your success and expertise in the market.

Do not forget to periodically re-tap the people in your inner circle. As you gain experience, they need to be brought up to date on your advances in knowledge and experience so they can continue as effective ambassadors. We have learned in our consulting with clients that their research shows that some prospects and even some current clients are not always aware of a new service the firm is offering.

Set a goal to connect with clients regularly. Whether currently involved in an active project with your team or not, clients want to hear from you. Just as you are constantly looking for new projects, they are also constantly looking for new expertise. They want to know that you, as their designer, are keeping abreast of new products and techniques and that you understand the value of those discoveries and how they meet ongoing needs.

Finally, but certainly not the last consideration in networking, is the enthusiasm and professionalism of your staff in representing the firm's public face or brand day-to-day. From a competent and warm reception at the front desk to a professional response by all team members to client's needs, the firm's strong commitment to high quality, personalized service is reinforced.

DATABASE MANAGEMENT

You must maintain information on and communicate with audiences. Tell everyone you are in business. The following story relays a powerful lesson about staying in touch with our public.

> Former Speaker of the United States House of Representatives Tip O'Neill told a story about his first campaign for Cambridge City Council, which he lost. While he received a tremendous vote in the other sections of the city, he realized he took his own neighborhood for granted. A Mrs. O'Brien, one of his high school teachers who lived across the street, told him the night before the election that she was going to vote for him even though he had not asked her to. He said "I've lived across from you for 18 years. I cut your grass in the summer. I shovel your walk in the winter. I didn't think I had to ask for your vote." "Tom," she replied, "let me tell you something: people like to be asked." From that point on, and throughout his entire career, every election day he would ask his wife Millie for her vote. She would always reply, "I'll give you every consideration."
>
> From *Man of the House* by Thomas P. O'Neill Jr., copyright © 1987 by Thomas P. O'Neill Jr. Used by permission of Random House Inc.

If you do not have contact management software in place, research and select the software that will best serve your needs for maintaining contact with clients, prospects, professional societies, media outlets, etc. Contact management software will allow you to code entries by vertical market, location, and expertise, rank prospects on the courtship continuum, and take advantage of certain sorting functions to select clients, prospects, influencers, community leaders, media outlets, professional societies, geographic area, market, and other data that serves your marketing needs.

Keeping a database up-to-date is a constant challenge so it is helpful to have a person in charge and to establish regular reviews for updating by all staff. We suggest that all staff learn how to load business card information into the database and that they do so within 24 hours of receiving them or that they religiously forward new information to a point person who is committed to loading information each day. If appropriate, conduct an internal seminar to educate employees on the intricacies of your database software and the how to's of entering information in the way that you want it. Set protocol not only for entry but also for follow-up with prospects.

Project managers are often the greatest source of database information in a design firm as they sit squarely in the middle of a project and deal with the myriad people involved in a project, from the influencers to the contractors who are getting things done on site. Cooperation from project managers in sharing personnel and time line changes that evolve over the life of a project is appreciated by every marketing team.

DATABASE IS A TOP PRIORITY

The following is a sample of the tactics a firm that concentrates on the educational market used to revamp and update the prospect section of their database.

- Determine who is already in the database. There may already be a gold mine of prospects, decision makers, and influencers in your database.
- Add to it. You always know more people than you think you do.
- Find additional decision makers. Review your targeted prospects for the names of decision makers: facilities, buildings, and grounds managers; campus planners; finance and administration leaders. Add to database.
- Find additional influencers. Think about the people you know on boards at the schools you attended and that your children attend: alumni, admissions, members of the boards of trustees, and others who are focused on future design projects. Add to database.
- Research your alma mater. Ask your staff to research their schools to learn of need for new buildings and renovations.
- Determine who else can carry your message. Stay in touch with your partners: vendors, consultants, and construction companies.
- Track people in new positions. Because new people often want to contract with new people, watch for promotions and new hires at your targeted schools.
- Keep the database up-to-date. Beyond the regular review of your database, use return receipt requests on your direct mail and bounce backs on e-mail to clean the database.
- Review current database codes. Determine if your codes are still relevant, if retrieval is easy, and if you need to add new codes.
- Learn about capital campaign cycles. Note important dates on the marketing calendar and determine how and when to get involved.

From our inner circle of friends and relatives, we all have a significant personal database, and as we develop business and community contacts via current, past, and prospective clients, vendors, and contractors, our professional database continually expands. Use your database to tap everyone on a regular basis because you never know who will bring you a lead or offer you a contract. We often hear people say they heard of something by word of mouth, but we may not think in terms of how that word of mouth got started—you!

DIRECT MAIL

A direct mail campaign may be scheduled as a monthly or quarterly event. All effort is focused on a targeted audience, so as you create your marketing plan for the year, think about which projects, which vertical market, or which knowledge you want to focus on and review your database for contacts in the targeted sector. If you feel that your database is lacking, consider purchasing member lists from appropriate professional organizations or direct mail lists that focus on specific criteria such as ZIP code or industry.

It is said that people take about 15 seconds to look at any document, so every direct mail piece you send needs to take that into account to capture readers' attention. Determine which projects best showcase your design work, both visually and in your case history, and use those precious seconds to send an enticing message that clearly states your expertise and your ability to solve problems in language that signals you understand and have successfully met the challenges the prospect is facing. Many direct mail campaigns feature a call to action. For designers, that might mean your captivating piece will feature an invitation to a firm-sponsored seminar or building tour.

The budget for a direct mail campaign includes the cost of writing copy, acquiring photography, designing the layout, printing, and postage. Your budget will adjust up or down according to the number of pieces mailed, but remember that the point of the effort is to introduce your expertise and celebrity and warm people up to the idea of calling you for services.

As with the press release, the work is not yet done because the direct mail often elicits the best result when it is followed up with a phone call. Always keep a copy of the specific database for each mailing with phone numbers. When follow-up is required, decide who will be the best person to make the call based on the relationship with the contact. It may be that a marketing assistant can do the follow-up, or you may want to designate Vertical Market Leaders, project managers, or other staff members to make selected calls. (Follow-up calls are often an opportunity to obtain additional contact names, so be prepared to record and pass new information along to the marketing staff.)

PRESENTATIONS

You replied to the Request for Proposals and you made the short list. Now you have an invitation to make a presentation that will convince the prospect to award the contract to you. Do you feel that this is a tall order? Preparing for presentations demands a mini-marketing plan of research, strategy, positioning, and goals as well as a timetable for production of graphic materials. Once you understand the prospect's challenge, look to your Book of Knowledge for the depth of information you need to win over the prospect. From pinstripes to tweed, know your audience and their needs, and then direct your comments and your expertise to them and direct your solution to their design challenge.

Your research on the prospects you are presenting to will tell you what they are looking for, what vehicles you should use to relay your expertise to them, and how your expertise relates to their needs. In a presentation, you will only give the information that the prospect needs to know. But you have to speak their language. If an education prospect asks about your experience with smart classrooms, you need to be able to talk about the subject clearly and thoroughly. Further, you must express the benefits of working with your team, and tell how you manage projects and solve problems. Your conclusion will be a brief summary of the "I've got it…" mantra. Finally, always be prepared to leave something behind that reinforces what you stated. One of our client firms has developed a very successful approach in its presentations. Their agenda includes time for both their designers and the prospects to not only discuss but also sketch solutions during the presentation, such that the prospect leaves the presentation with the sense that they have already started working with that design firm.

CHAPTER CONCLUSION

Now that you know what tools you have at your disposal and you have evaluated your current marketing materials, we will head into Chapter Eight to pull together all the strategies that you have listed from the previous chapters.

STRATEGIES: HOW WILL YOU GET THERE?

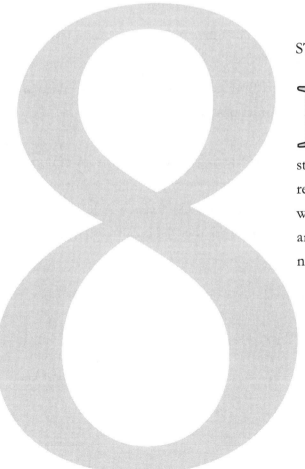

STRATEGIES SUPPORT YOUR GOALS

From your work in the previous chapters, you see how strategies spring from your research and from your goals. We want to ensure that strategies grow from your research because this is how research directly shapes the marketing plan, and we want to make sure you have catalogued all the strategies and tied them to the goals you set in Chapter Six. So now, review the various sources of your strategies.

- **Goals Worksheet:** Used to brainstorm strategies to correspond with the goals you set. You will match all your strategies from all the chapters against those goals. (Keep in mind, if a strategy is not tied to a goal, there is no reason to put it on your To-Do List.)

- **Vertical Market Worksheet:** Produced strategies like naming a Vertical Market Leader, joining a particular professional society, attending a conference, or ordering and reading an industry newsletter.

- **SCOT Worksheet:** From the recorded strengths, challenges, opportunities, and threats mentioned in your research, you brainstorm strategies to address what you learned.

- **Target Market Effectors:** Strategies may result from your firm's rankings on awareness, attitude, trial, and retrial.

- **Communication Audit and Publicity Questionnaire:** Both help identify gaps and overlaps in your communications that require strategies to make corrections in your programs.

You may have also gleaned strategies from evaluating your marketing materials and from ranking your prospects on the courtship continuum. Later in this chapter we will show you additional strategies you may not yet have thought of or included in the worksheet. First, let's take a look at how ABC Design fleshed out its Goals Worksheet with corresponding strategies from the work they did on all of these sources.

Goals Worksheet ABC Design		
Goal	Strategy	Tactic
In One Year:		
Implement strategic marketing plan	-Hire, assign marketing team -Create tracking system -Create Book of Knowledge, decide knowledge to add -Review budget	
Increase revenue in strongest vertical market (Sr. Living) by 10%	-Review fee structure for senior living market -Research senior living project opportunities -Increase contract values -Communicate emphasis on senior living projects to prospects, clients and the public.	
Expand geographically and secure first major senior living project in new geographic area	-Research opportunities -Build new networks -Media blitz to communicate ideas, showcase expertise via case histories	

Goals Worksheet ABC Design		
In Two Years:	Strategy	Tactic
Recruit additional (best) talent	-Assign recruitment team -Attend ALFA, AHCA conferences	
Build sustainability into firm culture	Educate current and recruit new talent	
Offer clients high tech know how	-Educate current and recruit new talent - Obtain testimonial. Use term "problem solvers" in case history.	
Secure clients who value design and high quality client service	Raise awareness of expertise through publicity campaign to target market	
Increase revenue by 10%	-Review current markets and adjust projections -Review fee structure for all markets -Communicate renewed focus to past and present clients, and prospects	
Strengthen our position in the regional market (senior living)	-Update regional public on ABC knowledge and experts -Target specific media outlets and reporters	

Now we are moving to the final level of effort on the SCOT Worksheet. Here we see the original ABC Design SCOT Worksheet from Chapter Three with the final column, Strategies, added and completed.

SCOT + S Worksheet ABC Design					
	Strengths	Challenges	Opportunities	Threats	Strategies
Depth of Knowledge		"Firm is not tracking knowledge to best effect."			-Create more efficient tracking system. -Create Book of Knowledge. Decide knowledge to add.
Scope of Services			Staff cited by client as good problem solvers.		Get testimonial. Use term "problem solvers" in case history.
Communication Skills		Audience not aware of firm's entire knowledge			Raise awareness of expertise through publicity campaign to target market.
Leadership	"Project manager led the entire team very well."				Disseminate (via e-mail to our market) expertise using case history and client testimonial.

Design Team	Area award-winning sustainable design				Use this in publicity campaign.
Fees			Revise (increase) firm wide fee structure		Review fee structure for all markets.
Portfolio			Client stated, "Your design work is better than you represent."		Increase budgets for photography and presentations. Revamp materials to reflect level of work. Ensure consistent message of ability.
Promotional Package				Competition from regional design firms.	Show our stuff better than the competition. Continue to build our presentations, proposal system, communications.
Proposals		Marketing efforts are reactive, not proactive.			Research prospects who need our expertise. Widen search for RFPs and increase number of monthly proposals.

Now that you have incorporated all the strategies culled from the discussions in the book to this point, we want to review some other key strategies you may not be aware of but that will help build awareness of the knowledge possessed by your firm, personally brand your employees, and bring prospects to the altar.

STRATEGY: CREATE MINI-MARKETING PLANS FOR EACH VERTICAL MARKET

Sometimes the corporate marketing plan can seem too big to digest, so it is helpful to see it broken down by vertical market. This is what the Vertical Market Worksheet: a mini-marketing plan for each of your vertical markets. This approach allows you to narrow your focus to promoting and selling a particular building type, to shepherding junior talent into eventual roles as leaders of that vertical market, and to going as deep as possible to penetrate the market.

STRATEGY: CREATE THE ONE-PROSPECT MINI MARKETING PLAN

To accomplish the goal of gaining a new client, we highly recommend creating a mini-marketing plan focused on bringing in the prospect as a client. We have seen this strategy used to great effect. An example is of a designer who coveted a relationship with a particular educational institution but who lost out to a competitor on his first try to win a contract. When the institution announced a second project, the designer created a mini-marketing plan to go after the project. He had his goal and set his strategies and tactics based on his research. He learned that the school preferred that all interested parties take a campus tour, something he neglected to do the first time around. Also, the school proposed a presentation format that they wanted all designers to follow closely; something that our client did not realize during his first presentation. The educational prospect was clearly looking for more interpersonal communication with the prospective designer. This time, our client completed essential research, took the tour, changed his presentation format, and got the job.

So how do you do that? Create a Dream Client List and think back to Chapter Four and how you ranked your prospects on the Courtship Continuum. How close are your current prospects to becoming signed-on clients? As we recommended, look first at those you have been "engaged" to and brainstorm what would bring them to "yes." The process will be different for each prospect. You know best what it will take to develop the relationship that will make it happen. The key is taking the time to strategize one prospect at a time, writing the simple one-sheet strategic plan, and assigning to your Knowledge Leader/Director of Marketing the responsibility to see that the strategies are carried out.

You can specifically assign the Marketing Coordinator the responsibility for researching the prospects on the list and matching their needs with firm knowledge so that an effective pitch can be made. Assign the responsibility for contacting specific prospects with the goal of arranging a principal-level meeting. Before the meeting occurs, review and rehearse the potential pitch; at the close of the meeting, the principal should suggest an action step that will move the relationship along the Courtship Continuum to the next level of potential project development. That step could be the suggestion of a visit to your firm, to a similar completed project, or to walk a potential site together. Back at the office, do a post-mortem and decide who will follow up, a principal or a Vertical Market Leader, and ensure a smooth handoff.

STRATEGY: PERSONALLY BRAND YOUR DESIGNERS

Once you have clarified your firm's Book of Knowledge and your designers' areas of expertise, work with designers on preparing for panel discussions, teaching opportunities, media interviews, and writing columns for industry publications. Include mention of your firm-wide and individual designers' expertise in all your marketing materials, especially on your Web site. Create what is essentially a Speakers Bureau List that can be used to promote your designers and their topics. A complete promotional package will include resumes or biographies, headshots, and sample writing on their topic.

STRATEGY: BUILD RELATIONSHIPS

It is no secret that one of the greatest differences between competitive firms today is the firms' employees and the relationships they build. As valuable as networking is, what we are talking about goes beyond networking to building warm relationships with your clients, within your profession, with your community. Working with and learning from your colleagues, enjoying what you do, and stepping up to a leadership position in your community are all part of effective marketing.

STRATEGY: USE PROFESSIONAL DEVELOPMENT BUDGET TO GROW FIRM KNOWLEDGE

Back in the research chapter, you assessed your knowledge and noted whether you needed to beef up your knowledge in a vertical market. Here is where you link your strategy with that finding. And this is a great reminder of two ideas: marketing and professional development are inextricably tied together, and you want to continually invest in your two greatest assets on your balance sheet, your knowledge and your employees.

STRATEGY: USE PROFESSIONAL SOCIETIES TO BUILD AWARENESS

We believe participation in professional societies is absolutely critical to becoming the go-to experts. These organizations are at the forefront of new knowledge in their industries and provide almost infinite opportunities to their membership to gain new information. You can use them to share what you know with your peers and the vertical market. Once you research the professional societies in your vertical market, choose the one with which you want to be involved. Let the society know of your interest in being involved and inquire about opportunities such as writing for their newsletter or speaking at their conferences. Learn how and when to approach them to take advantage of these opportunities by learning the editorial calendar (i.e., the theme and deadline for each issue) for publications and the expectations for word count. When your designers speak or write about their knowledge in any venue, communicate this to your clients and prospects.

STRATEGY: HARNESS WORD OF MOUTH, UPSELL CLIENTS, FIND AMBASSADORS FOR YOUR BRAND

Marketing is everyone's job, so involve everyone in the game. You can unleash the horsepower of your entire firm by getting buy-in from all employees. Present the marketing plan to them and keep them involved throughout the year by communicating marketing news, successes, and failures to them first. Employees should always be carrying the message and should not first hear of news that affects the success of the firm positively or negatively from outside the firm. It may be obvious to say this, but if you and your employees do not tell your story, no one will!

We all know that it is less expensive to keep an existing client than to find a new one. It is even more cost effective if the initial expenditure nets us not only one committed lifelong client but perhaps three new friends. Most of us know instinctively that word of mouth is the single most powerful form of marketing communication. And within the design industry, its impact on the success of firms is quite impressive. Your conversations with clients are the basis for marketing your brand. You need to influence word of mouth and harness it. Use staff and clients as ambassadors for your brand. Make every effort to bring everyone on board with your marketing plan.

STRATEGY: POSITION YOUR FIRM FOR SUSTAINABILITY

In today's market, sustainability adds value on all projects. Add to your knowledge base by joining "green" associations, attending their conferences, reading green publications and becoming LEED® (Leadership in Energy and Environmental Design) certified. Insert links on your Web site to inform readers of green trends and affiliations such as LEED®. Look at the history of sustainable architecture and take an inventory of your firm's involvement with sustainability, from solar houses of the 1960s and '70s onward. You may be surprised to find many examples of sustainability in your firm's past that you can now herald.

STRATEGY: MARKET TO PARTNERS—PAST, PRESENT, AND POTENTIAL

Look at the companies you have paired with in the past or are currently working with. How did you market to them? How have you kept them up-to-date about your evolving knowledge and interest in future partnerships? Are you considering partnerships with prospects or industry consultants and marketing to them, as well?

STRATEGY: CREATE A PLAN FOR ECONOMIC DOWNTURN

If you keep your finger on the pulse of your markets, you will be prepared for all that is coming at you. If one market is in a downturn, think about what is happening in other markets that you can take advantage of to fill potential voids. This could include smaller, more specialized projects in slower markets that involve your specialized areas of knowledge in sustainability, accessibility, or high-tech upgrades. Or it may mean that you must mount a campaign to move into a new, more profitable arena.

TAKING STRATEGIES TO THE NEXT STEP: TACTICS

Your goals are set and you have developed strategies. Now you are ready for the final part of the equation: tactics. Tactics are the step-by-step actions assigned to a particular person within a timetable and are the activities that fill up your To-Do List as shown in Chapter 10. Tactics are the manageable, bite-size chunks of daily effort that bring forth the achievement of goals. Begin by looking at your Goals Worksheet that now has strategies listed and brainstorm the tactics to fulfill each of the strategies. Time consuming? Yes! But, this is the essence of the To-Do List.

Taking just two of the ABC Design goals and corresponding strategies, we will develop the appropriate tactics. (The final step, which we will cover in Chapters Nine and Ten, is to assign tactics to specific individuals with a deadline for completion.)

Goal One is to improve revenue percentage from ABC's strongest vertical market, senior living, by 10% in one year. ABC Design knows that revenue from its two primary markets, senior living and healthcare, is almost equal, but that work effort is not equal. Staff is working harder to satisfy healthcare clients than senior living clients. Market forecasts report that the starts of senior living communities will continue to increase and although healthcare renovation contracts will hold strong, building starts for new hospitals will fall off over the next two years. Therefore, ABC is setting a goal of changing the revenue percentages from 50% - 50% to 60% senior living and 40% healthcare. The time is right for the firm to seize the opportunity to aggressively shift time and talent into the stronger, growing senior living market.

Goal Two is to expand geographic territory. Due to the nationwide demand for senior living communities, ABC Design is considering extending its geographic area. Issues to consider are travel time and administrative accommodations for long distance project management, budget increases, and expanded marketing efforts. In a wider market area, whether a regional or national increase, more effort will be required to maintain professional relationships, preserve coveted networking resources, and effectively get the job done when contracts do come to ABC.

Goals Worksheet ABC Design		
Goal	Strategy	Tactic
In One Year:		
Increase revenue in strongest vertical market (senior living) by 10%	-Review fee structure for senior living market -Research senior living project opportunities -Increase contract values -Communicate emphasis on senior living projects to prospects, clients, and the public.	-Vertical Market Leader to report on current project status in each market. -Vertical Market Leader and Knowledge Leader to continue updates on potential projects in each market. -Vertical Market Leader to reconnect with past clients and prospects in senior living market. -Knowledge Leader to prepare an e-mail campaign publicizing the firm's abilities and successes in senior living market.
Expand geographically and secure first major senior living project in new geographic area	-Research opportunities -Build new networks -Media blitz to communicate ideas, showcase expertise via case histories	-Vertical Market Leader to review database for networking sources. -Principal and Vertical Market Leader to get on the phone and on the road. -Accounting staff to review and report on estimated budget increases. -Knowledge Leader to mount campaign to communicate ABC has expanded territory. -Marketing Coordinator to research and report on most immediate contract opportunities.

COMMUNICATION WORKSHEET

In Chapter Four, we recommended that you complete a Communications Audit, and we did so for ABC Design to determine what they were currently doing to reach their public. You can also use that same worksheet and information to plan your communication campaign for the future since it is invaluable as a method of ensuring that you are focused on all your audiences, that you are communicating the right messages to them in the vehicles they are paying attention to, and that you are doing it on a regular schedule. As we said, it is a great way to get a quick yet thorough look at gaps or duplications in your communication efforts.

In your research with clients and prospects, you learned what their problems or challenges are and what they read, watch, listen to, belong to, and attend. Now you can develop communications to address that. By reviewing the positioning messages you worked on in Chapter Five and the knowledge you distilled into story ideas, you will develop the most convincing message for the selected audience. Remember that the best messages are the ones that speak the language of the recipient and reference the solutions you offer: "I know what you want and I've got it." Review all your vehicles for consistency and make any necessary adjustments to maintain your graphic design standards and highlight your message.

As far as frequency is concerned, we have helped firms organize successful four-time-a-year direct mail campaigns and 12-time-a-year press release schedules. You want to choose what will work best for you and your audiences and what you can sustain easily. Once you have filled out the Communication Worksheet, you can put everything in chronological order using the Frequency column and then transfer the tasks to your To-Do List.

CONCLUSION

With the endless exciting strategies you thought of to this point, the most important thing to do before you leave this chapter is to prioritize which strategies are most important. Then when you get to the next chapter where you will assign tasks and to the chapter after that where you will set deadlines, you will be able to fit all that is most important into your current schedule and push out the less significant strategies and tactics to the next year.

MOVE EASILY FROM ONE MARKET TO ANOTHER

TIP: FOCUS ON KNOWLEDGE FIRST, THEN ON THE MARKET SERVED

By focusing on knowledge first rather than on a vertical market, you remain open to the possibilities of applying various aspects of your expertise to more than one vertical market.

TIP: TAILOR YOUR KNOWLEDGE TO A SPECIFIC VERTICAL MARKET

Learn the needs of a specific market and marry those needs to your knowledge. Show how your knowledge could solve that market's biggest problem.

STAFF: WHO WILL DO THE WORK?

DEVELOPING THE MARKETING STAFF

An essential consideration for developing a marketing staff is that those who are involved in the marketing process have the expertise required, enjoy doing it, and receive the support they need. In this chapter, we will cover the organization of the marketing team, the roles and job descriptions for those who orchestrate and carry out the marketing plan, and the percentage of time both management and staff should expect to spend on marketing.

We propose the following organization chart of leadership: the Principal in Charge of Marketing takes the lead in the broad-based marketing decisions of the firm; the Knowledge Leader who in most firms is known as the Director of Marketing, oversees knowledge management and dissemination and manages the development and execution of the marketing plan; the Vertical Market Leader manages the knowledge associated with a specific market and is assigned to execute specific strategies to reach stated goals; the marketing coordinator, marketing assistant, and graphic designer perform the myriad daily tasks associated with reaching stated goals—that is, many of those tactics that repeatedly appear on the To-Do List; and all employees, whether designers, technical support, or administrative, carry the marketing message in all their professional and community activities and communications. Depending on the size of your firm, you may have a varied number of people involved in marketing or you may rely on just one person. There are roles to be played even though the actual title may vary and the same person's name may be listed next to one or more roles. No matter the scenario, the thing to remember is that all the work has to get done.

EMPOWERING THE ENTIRE TEAM

Naming a Knowledge Leader who has a solid commitment to stated marketing goals is one half of the formula for success. The other half is that the entire firm—from owner to designers to administrators to technicians—is also fully committed to the marketing goals. When annual marketing goals are determined, set individual marketing goals for employees (bring in one new client, secure two renovation contracts, attend two professional conferences) and incorporate those goals into performance reviews. Determine how accomplishment of goals will be measured and how success will affect employee compensation. Building strong and positive relationships is not limited to leaders and managers. The entire staff, through their areas of expertise and in their community activities, continually builds personal relationships with clients and prospects.

Use firm-wide office meetings to promote the activities and responsibilities of the marketing team to the entire staff so each employee has a sense of familiarity and ownership of the success of the marketing efforts and, thus, of the firm. Each person must have a full understanding of the breadth of the firm's knowledge and expertise and must be able to communicate your positioning message to your audience.

Marketing requires confidence, passion, and energy and although the ultimate success of your marketing plan will be on the shoulders of the Knowledge Leader, motivating your entire team will once again reinforce the elevation of your two greatest assets—your firm's knowledge and your employees—and will set you apart from the competition. Marketing your firm with your well-informed personalities via an organized and comprehensive plan will establish a firm foundation of strong clients and interesting, profitable projects.

Involve the entire staff in brainstorming sessions for effective marketing strategies, messages, and vehicles. Use the following list as a guideline of ways to constantly strengthen the ability and commitment of the entire team to carry the message.

- Empower employees to carry your message by communicating the marketing plan and revenue goals to all.
- Schedule seminars to discuss the message and how to deliver it most effectively.
- Communicate research information about client and prospect perceptions.
- Communicate revenue goals to employees.
- Share information about prospective work and vertical market statistics.

- Focus on marketing as an investment rather than an expense.

- Set goals for each employee's participation in achieving marketing goals and incorporate stated responsibilities into performance reviews and compensation.

- Involve the entire staff as a primary audience and sounding board for marketing messages, as radar for research efforts, as project team members who can learn and grow in their vertical market, and as participants in receiving and sharing firm knowledge.

ROLES OF THE MARKETING TEAM

We are providing general descriptions of the roles and responsibilities of the staff positions in a marketing team. You can also research job descriptions in human resources reference books as well as online or through human resources consultants. Human resources software that features job descriptions is available for purchase and you can also request job descriptions from your professional association.

PRINCIPAL IN CHARGE OF MARKETING

In general, design firm owners manage the marketing activities in their small to medium-sized firms. These entrepreneurs are confident in their abilities, and that confidence is widely acknowledged and appreciated by their audience. Individual personality and energy are key factors in marketing as these owners meet influencers, identify prospective clients, and ultimately bring signed contracts to the table. As their firms grow in expertise, recognition, project size, and profitability, many hours are spent in the community as one-on-one contacts with current and past clients, influencers, and professional contacts.

Entrepreneurs often enjoy great success by concentrating on the inside of their concentric circles for a number of years. Some percentage of new work will come to the firm through responses to requests for proposals and from referrals and alliances with other firms, but generally, contracts are written because of closely held loyalties.

Having a Principal in Charge of Marketing at the top of the organization chart is essential for several reasons. The number one reason is that an owner should have the final say in overarching marketing decisions such as the mission of the firm, which vertical markets to pursue, goals to be set, budgetary commitments, and the level of ability in the firm. Day-to-day decisions inherent to managing the marketing plan and the marketing team are the responsibility of the Knowledge Leader/Director of Marketing.

One person must remain in charge of the marketing or knowledge management, and as firms grow larger, that person may be someone other than an owner. This transition of leadership often occurs because the owner recognizes that due to growth it is not possible to manage all segments of the business—people, projects, marketing, and finances. That is when a Knowledge Leader comes in as the person in charge of managing the marketing and the firm-wide knowledge.

KNOWLEDGE LEADER/DIRECTOR OF MARKETING

The Knowledge Leader/Director of Marketing reports to the Principal in Charge of Marketing and has the primary responsibility for the overall marketing plan, the management of the marketing team, and the execution of all marketing tasks. The Knowledge Leader spends 100% of the time on marketing, from big-picture decisions to daily tactics, and sees that the team performs all marketing tasks on time. There is some discussion within the design industry as to whether marketing directors must be trained as designers in order to successfully sell the product. We feel the most critical element is the chemistry of the team and propose that a person with an extensive marketing background who fits in with the chemistry of the marketing team and the philosophy of the firm will bring success to the marketing effort.

The Knowledge Leader must be a good manager and must be comfortable presiding over the weekly marketing meeting. This meeting not only focuses on completed tasks and those to be accomplished but also on the reasons tasks are not moving forward. The Leader has the responsibility to work with the Principal in Charge of Marketing to set annual goals for marketing and knowledge management.

The Knowledge Leader works with the marketing team to establish and update Book of Knowledge folders, knows how your knowledge is currently used, how it should be used, and how it can be distilled into story ideas and disseminated to the marketplace via the vehicles your prospects and clients are paying attention to, listening to, and reading. The Knowledge Leader focuses on strengthening internal marketing systems, setting realistic deadlines, and monitoring the To-Do List.

The Knowledge Leader will see that all materials (including proposals, awards submissions, newsletters, case histories, etc.) are produced but will rely on a Marketing Coordinator or Marketing Assistant to do the actual production and will oversee database management but, again, will rely on staff to do the data input and run selected reports. The Leader will coordinate photography and the image archiving and will often attend on-site photo sessions. The Leader will develop story ideas, write press releases, and task the staff to coordinate distribution of media kits. The Knowledge Leader will also coordinate staff training as necessary for presentations and interviews and for speaking and writing assignments.

This position requires excellent management, organizational, and writing skills along with the ability to manage multiple deadlines. An extensive marketing background is essential, and previous experience in the design industry is helpful.

VERTICAL MARKET LEADERS

Each vertical market needs a named leader who knows the market. That means having the expertise to perform at a high level within the market, knowing the players and prospects in the market, and being positioned for recognition both internally and externally as an expert in that market. At this time, we are not discussing Vertical Market Leaders' project management duties (which are substantial) but rather their *marketing* responsibilities as managers of critical markets and how that duty affects their job description and the overall marketing plan.

Naming Vertical Market Leaders, usually principals or associates in the firm, will put the growth of each market squarely on the shoulders of the professional designing for the market, with support from the rest of the marketing team. This level of responsibility demands that Vertical Market Leaders be excellent managers with passion for the firm and motivation to reach established goals. These leaders are good at sharing their knowledge with the design staff and the marketing team, with the intention of grooming others for eventual leadership. We estimate that those who serve primary markets will spend 15% of their time on marketing, including visiting prospects, maintaining membership in trade organizations and professional societies, attending selected conferences, and writing, lecturing, and serving on panels in their areas of expertise. We estimate that Vertical Market Leaders serving secondary markets will spend 10% of their time on these tasks.

VERTICAL MARKET LEADERS MUST:

- Be a Principal or an Associate in the firm.
- Be perceived as an external expert.
- Be a good administrative manager.
- Have motivation, passion, and energy.
- Delegate and be willing to groom junior staff.
- Act as mentor and cheerleader.
- Know the market, know the players, know who to prospect.

VERTICAL MARKET LEADERS' TIME, TASKS, AND CHALLENGES

The following information may be used as a guideline for the time, tasks, and challenges that Vertical Market Leaders accommodate in a year.

PRIMARY MARKET: DEVOTE 15% OF TIME

- Belong to two trade organizations and maintain leadership in one.
- Attend four market-related conferences.
- Exhibit at two conferences.
- Make three speaking appearances.
- Write six articles or columns.
- Read everything!
- Continually research prospects and projects, with assistance of marketing department.
- Visit 12 prospects.

SECONDARY MARKET: DEVOTE 10% OF TIME

- Belong to one trade organization and maintain visibility.
- Attend two market-related conferences.
- Make one speaking or panel appearance.
- Write three articles.
- Read top publications in the market.
- Conduct market research, with assistance of marketing department.
- Visit six prospects.

TERTIARY MARKET: DEVOTE 2.5% OF TIME

- Belong to one trade organization and be an active participant.
- Attend one market-related conference.
- Read market publications.
- Write for one market-related newsletter.

MARKETING COORDINATOR

The Marketing Coordinator is fully devoted to tasks related to the marketing plan and receives direction from the Knowledge Leader. Duties include performing market research and assisting the Knowledge Leader in the development and production of client presentations, proposals, awards submissions, and all collateral materials. The Marketing Coordinator will monitor industry publications and report on Requests for Proposals in selected markets and will monitor and archive news and publicity pieces about the firm. Knowledge of image and publishing software and hardware; good creative and technical writing skills; excellent communication, organizational, and analytical skills; and the ability to work under the pressure of deadlines are essential. The Coordinator will manage the Marketing Assistant.

MARKETING ASSISTANT

The Marketing Assistant also devotes 100% of the time to the marketing effort and takes direction from the Marketing Coordinator. Duties include maintaining the database and image library, preparing marketing reports and data for weekly meetings, restocking specialty needs and supplies for the marketing department, and providing administrative support to all members of the marketing team as needed, including assisting in the production of proposals and the preparation of special projects for the Vertical Market Leaders. The Assistant is a team player and a well-rounded administrator who has knowledge of image and publishing software and hardware, good technical abilities, good communication and organizational skills, and works well under the pressure of deadlines.

GRAPHIC DESIGNER

Whether you choose to have a graphic designer on staff or as a contracted consultant, this professional will create visual solutions to communicate your message in print and electronic media from logo to business cards to signage, will develop layout and production of brochures, awards submissions, presentation boards, and direct mail pieces, and will develop the Web site and multimedia projects. On-staff Graphic Designers will require up-to-date computer systems with graphics software and high-quality printers to produce their designs and create and maintain Web sites. The Graphic Designer receives direction from the Knowledge Leader/Director of Marketing.

BUSINESS DEVELOPMENT MANAGER

Medium to large firms with fully staffed marketing departments may also include a Business Development Manager who is responsible for identifying and developing relationships with prospective clients. The Business Development Manager spends 100% of the time on business development by working closely with the Principal in Charge of Marketing, the Knowledge Leader, and the Vertical Market Leaders. That team meets on a regular basis, usually weekly, to monitor the status of networking in each vertical market, to review requests for proposals, and to discuss contract opportunities. The Business Development Manager is a results-oriented, organized person who excites clients and prospects about the design firm and how its employees can meet their challenges and solve their problems.

CONCLUSION

In this chapter, we looked at how the entire marketing effort is staffed, and while designers are extraordinarily busy with projects, we see that it is critical that they lead their markets as branded experts. That personal branding is the key task of the Knowledge Leader/Director of Marketing who must have a strong sense of the expertise of the firm in each of its markets and understand the most effective methods for disseminating that knowledge. While that person must keep the reactive marketing process of responding to RFPs going, it is the proactive marketing and the personal branding that will bring some of the biggest successes to the firm. In the next chapter, as you look at the To-Do List, you will be inserting the names of your staff under "person responsible" and setting deadlines for all tactics.

THE TO DO LIST: WHAT IS THE SCHEDULE?

TAKING ACTION

Now is the time to convert the decisions and discoveries made in the previous chapters into action items. As you worked through all the worksheets, you established goals and brainstormed strategies. In Chapter Eight, you broke strategies down into tactics. Now we are at the point where the tactics go into the To-Do List as action items, with person responsible and assigned deadlines. We recommend having deadlines for each tactic leading up to a key deadline. As we say to our students in class, if you only record one deadline for landing on the moon on November 1, you will wake up on November 1 and not be on the moon. So, insert into your To-Do List every single task (with a completion date) required to get to the moon!

You will be able to use the To-Do List for a variety of purposes:

- **Annual Marketing Plan:** You will know what to expect in the weeks, months, and year to come.

- **Daily Schedule:** The To-Do List will provide an overview of what has to be accomplished by the marketing department each day. In addition to the tactics you have already listed, be sure to include your administrative tasks such as photo shoots, attendance at a conference or an in-house training program.

- **Meeting Agenda:** The person running marketing meetings can go around the room and check in with each attendee to learn if they are meeting their deadlines or if the deadlines need to change. During the meeting, tasks and deadlines can be revised and updated as action is taken.

- **Marketing Reports:** The historical information gleaned from the To-Do List helps to create weekly, monthly, quarterly, or annual marketing reports.

- **Next Year's Annual Marketing Plan:** You now have the perfect template that can be used year in and year out to create next year's plan, with modifications, of course. It is important to save your To-Do List. Do not delete items when they are completed, just check them off. That way, when you create your marketing plan for next year, you can simply modify deadlines (such as when to send out the quarterly newsletter, when to do the annual photo shoot of the staff, when to apply for a particular conference, etc.). You will not have to reinvent the wheel.

Keep in mind that deadlines cannot continually move out. Action needs to actually take place, and the tasks need to have a result. In some cases, the completion of a task may mean that it evolves into a new item with a new deadline. It is a living document that will grow and change as information is gathered and actions are decided upon.

Get started on your To-Do List by putting in all the tactics/action items you are already doing along with their deadlines. Then, move on to the new tactics you listed on the Goals Worksheet.

To-Do List	Date: 1/2	
Tactic/Action Item	Person(s) Responsible	Deadline

See: www.greenway.us/expertbook for this template

Now, let's take a look at the To-Do List ABC Design came up with as a result of its brainstorming session for first quarter of the year. The first thing you will notice is that ABC personalized its list by adding a column labeled Category. You may wish to personalize your list in some way for purposes of sorting information by various categories or to more fully describe the work product.

For purposes of discussion, ABC's To-Do List shows just the communication strategies for the first quarter. You can see that some deadlines do overflow into the second quarter. This will happen because

ABC Design To-Do List	Date:		
Tactic /Action Item	Person(s) Responsible	Category	Deadline
E-mail newsletter on a quarterly basis	Knowledge Leader, Graphic Designer, Marketing Assistant	Newsletter	3/31
Share knowledge with public monthly	Marketing Coordinator	Press Releases	1/28 2/28 3/28
Update Web site case histories and photos	Marketing Assistant	Web site	2/15
Take one client and one prospect to lunch	Vertical Market Leaders	Clients, Prospects	3/31
E-mail "knowledge news" of recent classes taken and seminars attended	Knowledge Leader, Marketing Coordinator	E-mail	2/28
Schedule info meeting for existing clients	Vertical Market Leaders	Meeting	4/30
Schedule seminar for prospects	Knowledge Leader, Principals, Vertical Market Leaders, Marketing Coordinator	Seminar	5/15
E-mail newsletter with story about new statewide building incentive	Knowledge Leader, Marketing Coordinator, Vertical Market Leader	Newsletter	3/15
Add Acme Building story to Web site	Marketing Assistant	Web site	3/15
Share knowledge with public through informal presentations across theregion	Knowledge Leader, Principals, Vertical Market Leaders	Presentations	4/15
Meet with regional developers	Principals, Vertical Market Leaders	Presentations	5/15

of in-house scheduling conflicts or availability of consultants or others involved in the completion of action items. Your To-Do List will be much longer and it will change as you regularly revisit it at your marketing meetings.

Over the years, we found it most helpful to revise the To-Do List globally only once a week, following discussion of each tactic at our weekly marketing meeting. From week to week, each person responsible for a tactic kept personal notes on progress and then received an updated version within a designated period after the weekly meeting and review. You, of course, will set the schedule and process that works best for you but we do recommend that you meet either weekly or bi-weekly. Keep one copy of each list in an archive so you can refer back to verify information for future planning or resolve questions that may arise.

> ### TIP: A WORD TO THE WISE
> The marketing process is one that develops over time and takes time. Results will come, but they will not be instantaneous. The goal is to plot a course that will produce desired results for the long term. Be prepared to establish valuable relationships, compile a useful database, produce marketing pieces that will sell your expertise, and most important, create project opportunities and success.

CONCLUSION

Once you have completed the entire marketing plan with all its research and goals, strategies and tactics, and have converted them to your To-Do List, we urge you to keep it out on your desk, on a clipboard, perhaps, and refer to it every day. Add to it, bring it to meetings, and make revisions as needed. From our experience, it is the one daily plan that does not end up on the shelf gathering dust!

BUDGET: HOW MUCH WILL IT COST?

CREATING THE BUDGET

In our discussion about goals, we stated that you should expect to reach or surpass a certain goal for total revenue each year and that you base your total expense budget, including the marketing budget, on that number. As you set your projected annual budget, you will spend considerable time analyzing each line item and may, if you are a young firm, allocate a best guess lump sum for marketing. Startup firms should rely on advice from their accountant, their professional society, and their professional peers. Each one of these resources will have facts and figures that can substantiate very good best guesses.

As your business expands and your marketing expertise grows, you will rely on your annual statistics to confirm actual numbers and will, in time, ask the Knowledge Leader/Director of Marketing to submit a fully itemized annual budget based wholly on experience.

MARKETING-TO-SALES RATIO

In the design industry, the marketing-to-sales ratio generally ranges from 5% to 15%, while some report as low as 3% and some as high as 18%. ABC Design uses 7%, including salaries, and lists all costs relating to conferences, seminars, speeches, and article writing under the line item "Professional Development" in the marketing budget. The Society for Marketing Professional Services (SMPS) notes that "It is highly likely that the majority of your marketing costs will be related to personnel" and suggests that once you come up with a percentage, consider adjusting it for a variety of situations. For example, subtract 2% to 3% if you have a high percentage of repeat clients, receive a high percentage of work from prime consultants, or have a highly experienced marketing team focusing on well-established markets. Conversely, add 2% to 3% if your collateral materials are being redone or if you are entering a new market. From our experience in the industry, we estimate that firms are generally in the 6% to 8% range. Each Owner, Principal in Charge of Marketing, and Knowledge Leader will have distinct ideas about budgeting and expenditures, and although there are certain accounting principals to heed, there is no right or wrong in the percentages, ratios, or line item allocations.

The following is an example of the ABC Design marketing budget based on its $4 million in annual income. In this budget, marketing salaries are allocated according to the percentage of projected time targeted to be spent on marketing tasks.

172

A reminder that, as you itemize and refine your budget, there will be vehicles that you will want to include—advertising in a particular media outlet, dues to a professional society, or attendance at an annual conference—but may find the cost too prohibitive. Put the information in the budget and mark no go on the line item. Plan to earn the money and expense it for the next year. In the meantime, stretch your budget by bootstrapping as often as you can.

ABC Design Annual Marketing Budget	Date 1/2			
Account	Item		Projected	Actual
New Market Venture* *Includes advertising campaign, attendance at two targeted conferences, prospect contact			35,000	
	Holiday card (in-house production)		500	
	Brochure		3,500	
	Post cards		1,000	
Software	Purchase Updates		500	
Photography			12,000	
Copying			3,500	
Web Site	Updates		2,500	
Awards	Fees/Design/ Production		3,000	
Events	Spring Fling		3,500	
Networking			1,200	

Professional Development	Seminars	2,500	
	Conferences	3,000	
Professional Association Dues		2,250	
Subscriptions		300	
Travel		4,000	
Telephone		3,000	
Postage	Holiday card	350	
	Post card	250	
	Administrative	1,200	
Office supplies		6,000	
SUBTOTAL		89,050	
MKTG SALARIES*		194,000	
* Vertical Market Leaders (2 primary 25,500 1 secondary 8,500 Knowledge Leader 65,000 Marketing Coor. 45,000 Graphic Designer 50,000			
TOTAL MKTG EXPENSES (Note: 7% of gross revenues)		283,050	

ALLOCATING SALARIES FOR MARKETING

How do you decide what percentage of time management and staff should spend on marketing and, therefore, what percentage of salaries to allocate to the marketing budget? Full-time marketing staff will be allocated 100% to the marketing salaries line item. The more challenging figure is what percentage of salary for non-marketing staff should be allocated. In the beginning, you will rely on a best guess, but after one year, data from your time management software will tell you more precisely the number of marketing hours and dollars expended by each employee. From our experience, we predict that a vertical market leader who manages a primary market may spend 15% of total time on marketing that arena, and a manager of a secondary market may spend about 10%. Therefore, if a vertical market leader earns $85,000, you know that you can allocate at least $12,750 to the marketing budget for a primary market and $8,500 for a secondary market.

During your annual review of all marketing activities, you can weigh the time and money spent on marketing against the overall success of your plan. Success in terms of wider recognition and increased

BOOTSTRAPPING, PIGGYBACKING, AND BARTERING

Bootstrapping refers to the innovative ways that many young firms run their business with little cash. For firms that are in the early years, there is no better way to get things accomplished than to make a determination about what you absolutely must pay for and what you can do inexpensively or through trade or barter. In the former category are the obvious administrative costs: salaries, utilities, and the need to pay for fabulous graphic design and photography. In the latter category, you can produce great business cards, letterhead, and envelopes inexpensively on your computer and you can save money by sending digital press releases instead of paying for the production of hard copy media packages.

Piggybacking refers to any innovative ways you "hitch a ride" to a place you can not afford to go to alone! The best example is going to important industry events as a guest of a member. Bartering refers to the ways individuals and firms trade with each other for an important service. Although we just mentioned the critical need to pay for fabulous graphic design and photography, some designers and photographers trade for those valued services.

contracts will be confirmation that your Vertical Market Leaders and marketing staff are working well together to promote the goals of your plan, and that the roles and responsibilities you assigned are on target. If you are not attaining new clients and revenue at the rate you projected, you will need to make proper adjustments in time, responsibilities, and goals.

RECORD KEEPING

Record keeping is a significant part of marketing. The statistics from tracking vertical markets, including clients, projects, and financial results as well as from tracking the results of each marketing effort, inform the budget decisions you will make for the next year. As you consider new line items to incorporate into

DEVELOPING AND REFINING THE MARKETING BUDGET

- Set in place annual planning, budgeting, and review process.
- Determine gross revenue and phasing of potential projects in each market.
- Determine marketing budget total and line items.
- Clarify with vertical market leaders their specific revenue goals and annual expenses per market.
- Determine who is responsible for the marketing budget (Principal in Charge, Knowledge Leader), including periodic reporting.
- Create a system of marketing department approval for expenditures.
- Review with accountant the annual projections in total and per vertical markets in anticipation of cash flow planning.
- Track annual revenue and expenses for each vertical market.
- Instruct staff how to allocate their marketing time and expenses on time sheets.
- Conduct monthly marketing sales review. Knowledge Leader convenes with Principal in Charge of Marketing, Business Development Manager, Vertical Market Leaders and in-house accountant.

your marketing plan—a wider advertising campaign, an updated Web site, additional staff—you can review the results and expenses related to past performance to assist in making decisions for the future. The marketing and accounting staff can work together to develop spreadsheets to track the costs of advertising and direct mail campaigns, photography, printing, Web site development, and marketing personnel. Look at marketing profit and loss figures on a regular basis, at least semi-annually, and adjust your marketing and overall budget accordingly.

SALES PROJECTIONS

The most important goal you set and must attain each year is your revenue projection. Every business needs a steady, adequate stream of cash coming in from satisfied clients. Thus, maintaining financial stability is an undeniable goal of every marketing effort and one of the primary purposes of marketing has always been to find people with reliable resources of cash who will spend it on your company.

It is imperative that you track sales and monitor whether your revenues are up or down each month. The marketing team needs to be fully aware of the level of urgency related to bringing in additional projects and revenues. The team must be prepared to report on which projects are the most likely to come in and when, as well as if there is a need to spend additional monies and personnel effort to bring contracts to closure.

Once again you can refer to your Vertical Market Worksheet as a tool. In this case, it can be used to make accurate sales projections. Looking back at your marketing history is a way you can predict the future of your marketing success and your sales projections. Use your completed Vertical Market Worksheet as the basis for discussing potential in each of your primary and secondary markets and make the most accurate sales projections by considering the following.

- Review research on industry growth projections for each vertical market (primary, secondary, and tertiary, if applicable).

- Discuss your prospects for annual growth in each vertical market and how growth will affect staffing.

- Review sales results from past years in total and for each vertical market.

- Review sales to date for current fiscal year and compare to the annual sales projection. If down from amount estimated, consider how to adjust for current and coming year.

- Review fees predicted to come in before year end.

- Build potential contracts from the ground up by reviewing your list of prospects and noting those who are closest to the altar (see Courtship Continuum in Chapter Four).

- Estimate on each potential project the expected revenue and expected receipt of first payment.

- Review cash flow for the current and past two years to detect patterns of highest and lowest income activity. Use this information to think about how to improve cash flow in the slowest months.

CONCLUSION

Now that you have discussed and completed the marketing budget, we are ready for the final topic, evaluation.

EVALUATION: HOW WILL YOU RECOGNIZE SUCCESS?

MEASURING SUCCESS

Some designers say, "We're making money, so we must be successful." Maybe that is true, maybe not. As we stated at the very beginning, money is important. You must set financial goals and attain them because you need financial resources to stay in business, but there are other measures of success to consider such as satisfied clients, a national reputation, celebrity employees, receipt of awards, and peer recognition. Put your system in place, set your goals, establish your marketing team, do the research, implement your strategies, complete your tactics on deadline and then measure the results.

To recognize success, you have to be able to measure

it. For example, you may have set a goal to "improve marketing communications." You implemented strategies and completed tactics to broadcast the specific knowledge of a Vertical Market Leader to clients and prospects. When that employee is named by your audience as the go-to expert in the market, that is a measurable, successful result.

EVALUATION

Here are some questions to ask yourself as you attempt to evaluate your plan and where your firm is headed.

- **Communication:** Do the content and vehicles in your firm communications work effectively?

- **Target markets:** Do you have clearly agreed-upon target markets? Have you completed the research on market needs? Have you created a target market database for easy contact?

- **Positioning statement:** Does your positioning statement match your firm's strengths with market needs and an awareness of how your firm compares with the competition?

- **Goals:** Have you set realistic yet challenging goals?

- **Strategies:** Will the strategies you brainstormed accomplish the goals you set? Are they realistic for your staff to accomplish?

- **Finances:** Have you developed an adequate budget to make it all happen?

- **Knowledge:** Are you staying abreast of the marketplace?

REPORTING ON RESULTS

From your Book of Knowledge to your research to your profitability, you will want to report on specifics as well as overall results. By the nature of the design industry and with the help of great software, most firms have excellent financial, project, management, and marketing records. Analyzing the information may be more of a challenge but a challenge that needs to be met in order to truly evaluate success.

Reports on firm-wide activities from finances (accounting reports) to projects (profitability and status reports) to marketing (expense and evaluation reports, To-Do List) are your guide to critical decision making. These reports reveal opportunities worth pursuing and changes in markets that need to be addressed.

Evaluation of your marketing plan is an ongoing activity and should be on the table at every marketing meeting. Not only should you continually evaluate overall success, but you should also measure individual effort and accountability with the goal in mind of managing your marketing better, faster, and more economically.

The following are suggestions for using your regular marketing meetings to not only move forward with your plan tasks but to evaluate whether your plan is producing positive results through the accomplishment of your stated goals and taking you where you want to go. Review of the results and expenses related to past performance is imperative to making decisions for the future.

Weekly Marketing Meeting and Weekly Marketing Report

- Review To-Do List. Note completed tasks, review and reschedule outstanding tasks.

- Look at each vertical market and current activities in each. Trade show to attend? Speaking opportunities coming up? Press release to issue?

- Discuss prospects. Assess status of relationships, review mini-marketing plan for each prospect, and brainstorm additional approaches to new prospects as appropriate.

- Approve expenditure requests.

- Look to tasks and deadlines for week ahead to remind all of expectations.

Monthly Marketing Meeting and Monthly Marketing Report

- Review what was accomplished in previous month.

- Review monthly financial statement. Check budget against actual expenses and adjust as appropriate.

- Review prospects and lead development for projects.

- Discuss new knowledge and trends in industry and specific vertical markets.

- Discuss the next month's schedule.

Quarterly Marketing Meeting and Quarterly Marketing Report

- Review quarterly report which assesses status of long range goals and may designate changes to the original marketing plan, such as adjustments to personnel assignments, vertical market activities and budget requirements.

- Report on revenue and profitability, firm wide and within each vertical market..

- Determine status with current clients and prospects.

- Discuss reasons for win or loss on proposals, including client feedback.

- Review market trends in each vertical market and effect on firm.

- Review software for updates and new resources.

- Review To-Do List for last quarter and discuss to-do's for upcoming quarter.

Annual Marketing Meeting and Annual Marketing Report

- Report on revenue and profitability, firm-wide and within each vertical market.

- Determine if realistic yet challenging goals were set for the past year to obtain new business and how successes and failures affects the upcoming year.

- Determine if annual budget was adequate to make it all happen.

- Audit all current communications vehicles and make recommendations for modifications.

- Report on client feedback on overall project satisfaction and success in meeting client's needs.

- Detail how firm compares with the competition.

- Does current positioning statement match firm's strengths with market needs?

- Review trends in vertical markets, primary, secondary, and tertiary.

POST-OCCUPANCY EVALUATIONS

Research never ends, and that is true when it comes to project post-occupancy evaluations. We believe more design firms could use post-occupancy evaluations as a research tool and learning opportunity. Case histories and post-occupancy evaluations all tie together as part of client research. Client research increases the knowledge base of the firm and provides content for communications with clients, prospects, the community, and the media. Therefore, you must let clients know early on that you will be interested in using their project as a case history in firm-wide communications through vehicles such as the Web site, direct mail, and presentations and that you will want to conduct the comprehensive post-occupancy evaluation that documents the pertinent design and construction information about the project. This should be a part of initial contract negotiations so it is clear to all concerned that you will be looking for feedback on the project.

We encourage firms to set up a system for post-occupancy evaluations that ranks team performance, lessons learned, budget considerations, technical information, and quality of work. A post-occupancy checklist should include the following criteria and any other items that you deem necessary to enhance your project knowledge. As with all research questions, we emphasize the need for brevity. Just as in the research interviews, more people will be inclined to say yes to your request if you assure them that you will adhere to a stated time limit of 15 or 20 minutes.

INTERVIEW TOPICS FOR POST-OCCUPANCY EVALUATION

- Technical expertise of entire team and accuracy of plans.

- Quality of work.

- Communication

- Accuracy of cost estimates, budget, final construction costs, design, and consultant fees.

- Review of change orders, approval processes, and field problems.

- Ability of team to stay on schedule.

- Did client information and stated needs ultimately produce the desired outcome?

- Does the building serve its intended purpose?

- Is the building beautiful, efficient, public-friendly, secure, green, high-tech, or special in any other way?

When the evaluations are complete, you will have the comprehensive information needed to create case histories with testimonials from the client highlighting the success and uniqueness of the project and the lessons learned to add to your Book of Knowledge.

CONCLUSION: YOU'VE GOT IT!

One of the things we said in Chapter One is that often, firms go through the planning process, do the research, and write the marketing plan only for it to end up on a shelf. We have attempted to offer you a system that is thorough, sensible, and easy to execute, one that challenges you sufficiently such that your marketing plan will not sit on a shelf. Our hope is that you are now enthusiastic about not only executing your plan but actually managing your marketing.

To maximize your two greatest assets, your knowledge and your employees, and to carry out the two overarching strategies of managing your marketing and marketing your knowledge, you must oversee a well-oiled marketing machine. Let's first review how best to manage your marketing by strengthening and refining your system and then how best to manage your knowledge by strengthening and supporting your experts.

Manage Your Marketing

- **The Marketing Machine:** Take an inventory of all parts of the internal marketing system. How well organized is it? What still needs to be done? Estimate how long tasks will take, set realistic deadlines, and include them on the To-Do List.

- **Maintain Archives:** Keep case histories, with testimonials, up-to-date. Vertical Market Leaders are tasked with updating information on past and current projects in coordination with the Knowledge Leader so information can be continually added to the Story Idea Archive.

- Keep Image Archive up to date. Determine relevancy of older images and retire or renew. Schedule photography shoots as necessary for current work. Plan one year ahead for photography.

- **To-Do List:** Flesh out and manage the To-Do List. This is a living document and an ongoing challenge for the Knowledge Leader as information comes into the firm on a daily basis.

- **Assign Tasks:** As new strategies are incorporated into the To-Do List, make team members aware of new or changed assignments and deadlines through the weekly marketing meeting or on an individual basis. Entire team is held accountable for assigned marketing tasks.

- **Next Year's Marketing Plan:** Keeping the *To Do List* up-to-date throughout the year as tasks are added is invaluable for the creation of next year's plan.

- **Marketing Meetings:** Determine frequency of marketing meeting. Most firms meet weekly, but as the Knowledge Leader monitors tasks, deadlines, and completion, certain teams and individuals may need to meet on a more or less frequent basis.

- **Marketing Reports:** Provide regular reports on marketing that include accomplishment of marketing tasks and status of financial obligations. Be prepared with reports on whatever frequency your firm needs them: weekly, monthly, quarterly, or annually.

- **Review Work Methods:** Review how your firm finds and captures clients. Discuss research methods and determine level of success in finding prospects and clients. Review new industry trends and challenges and how firm can communicate abilities and solutions to prospects, clients, and influencers.

- **Review Capabilities Brochure:** Determine the purpose of a brochure and if you want to produce a print brochure along with your Web site. Set a timeline and determine distribution list.

- **Review Your Web Site:** Review on a regular basis and be certain that information is up-to-date, including graphic images. Link your Web site with appropriate associations and design-related sites.

- **Assess Current Direct Mail Program:** Decide if it effectively communicates the message that your firm is able to meet the needs of your clients and prospects.

- **Join Professional Societies:** Determine the best opportunities for design staff.

- **Attend Trade Shows and Conferences:** Attend and exhibit as appropriate.

- **Read Trade Publications:** Review publications for contacts, latest trends, and research information.

- **Speaking and Writing:** Take advantage of speaking and writing opportunities. Pitch appropriate employees as experts to the appropriate audience. Create a promotional package that offers speakers and writers with a list of current topics.

- **Maintain the Database:** Confirm that information about clients, prospects, influencers, professional societies, and media outlets is added to the database on a timely basis (within 24 hours is a good rule of thumb).

- **Manage the Annual Marketing Budget:** Once annual goals are set, the Knowledge Leader can determine what expenses are required to meet those goals, such as production and travel costs, the cost of development of new markets, and changes in percentage of salaries allocated to marketing. Maintain expense records. Assign a marketing team member to work with the accounting department to track expenses and pertinent historical statistics.

- **Work in Tandem:** Balance work that must be completed as soon as possible, such as proposals, with long-term strengthening of the system.

Manage Your Knowledge

- **Create a Book of Knowledge:** Ensure that all knowledge coming into the firm is captured and archived for easy retrieval.

- **Name the Leaders:** Demonstrate the value the firm places on knowledge by naming the head of Knowledge Management, the Knowledge Leader and the Vertical Market Leaders who track knowledge within the specific market and will write or speak about that knowledge. Train staff as necessary for presentation, interview, speaking, and writing assignments. Clarify who is monitoring what sources of information.

- **Assess Knowledge:** Determine gaps that need to be filled and promote professional development opportunities.

- **Distill Knowledge:** Develop story ideas that effectively communicate your message to your audience.

- **Disseminate Communications:** Inform staff first, then disseminate through press releases, seminars, e-mail blitz, columns, etc. Use communications vehicles your market is paying attention to for speaking, writing, and feature opportunities.

- **Continue Day-to-Day Research:** Clarify that all staff can act as radar for information from external sources. Create an expectation that staff will route that information to the Marketing Department on a regular basis.

- **Professional Societies:** Use membership and involvement in professional societies, trade shows, and conferences to gain new knowledge and to update your markets about new information.

GOOD LUCK!

GLOSSARY OF TERMS

This glossary provides definitions for terms used in marketing that may not be familiar to you and for the unique terms we apply in *Business Comes to the Expert*.

Book of Knowledge: Our short-hand way of referring to the knowledge possessed by your firm and its employees and the system you will use to categorize areas of expertise for easy dissemination. The topics in your Book of Knowledge will expand as new knowledge comes into the firm.

Bootstrapping, Piggybacking, and Bartering: These three terms are grouped together because they all represent ways to save money. Bootstrapping refers to the practice of getting things accomplished in business with minimal capital. Designing and printing letterhead and business cards in house is a common bootstrapping practice. An example of piggybacking is going as a guest to an organizational event when you cannot afford the annual membership. Bartering, or trading, your services for other services that you need works very well for designers.

Brand: Any name, symbol, or other identifier used to identify the goods or services of a seller that differentiate them from similar goods or services of competitors. It gives rise to expectations in the minds of consumers about the experience they will have of the product or service. The legal term is "trademark."

Case History: Also referred to as case studies, project histories, project synopses, or project closeout reports, this is an encapsulation of the critical elements of a completed design project. We recommend that it include the challenge or problem presented by the client, the recommendation by the design firm, and the result, which is often a client testimonial. Often contained on a single page and featuring a dynamic photograph, it is used to translate your knowledge into meaningful communications to your markets.

Celebrity: Refers to the recognition your employees gain when their expertise is put in the spotlight and disseminated to the public in appropriate vehicles.

Chemistry: The sense of excitement, like-mindedness, and cooperation that instantly connects people when they meet for the first time.

Client Testimonial: Brief quote obtained from clients about a job well done. It is a third-party endorsement that is used in communication vehicles as a verification or validation of designers' abilities and expertise.

Concentric Circles: An illustration about how to think about marketing. That is, to see the inner circle as the home base of your marketing and consecutive outer circles as opportunities to grow out beyond the inner circle while maintaining a strong hold on the base.

Courtship Continuum: Method used to rank and gauge your relationship with prospects.

Dissemination: The distribution of your knowledge to your audiences via selected communication vehicles.

Distillation: Refers to the process of taking your entire Book of Knowledge and translating and condensing it into bite-size pieces for easy dissemination to the market.

Elevator Speech: The slang term for a marketing technique in which a person has approximately 30 seconds, or the duration of an elevator ride, to inform or persuade an audience about a service or product.

Fountain of Content: Knowledge that flows into an organization, where it is stored, distilled, and disseminated out into various communication vehicles.

Knowledge Leader/Director of Marketing: The point person for both managing your firm's knowledge and managing your marketing. This person has the primary responsibility for the development and execution of the marketing plan, the production of all marketing reports, and the management of the marketing team.

Knowledge Management: The foundation of the marketing plan and the internal system in which knowledge is stored for easy retrieval, distilled into easily digestible pieces and regularly disseminated to specific audiences.

Media Kits: A collection of information that firms send to media outlets. They can include an interesting story idea, press release, and company information as well as suggestions about people who are available for interview and a fact sheet/"backgrounder," images, copyrights, captions, and credits. Many firms have kits "on the shelf" for routine media requests.

Media Outlets: Any newspaper, newsletter, magazine, radio, television, or Internet site that your firm uses to get the message to your market. The three types of media are trade, business, and consumer. In design, trade media refers to that which exclusively covers design and construction; business media refers to any outlets that focus predominantly on business news such as *Business Week* or *The Wall Street Journal*; and consumer media is everything else that you read, listen to, or investigate such as your daily paper, National Public Radio, or an Internet site.

Mission Statement: A brief description of a company's fundamental purpose. It answers the question, "Why do we exist?" and articulates the company's purpose both for those within the organization and for the public.

Positioning: The place your firm occupies in the mind of your audience.

Story Ideas: A term used in publicity to describe the brief pitch or the angle used to interest a reporter in a story. It is used in this context to emphasize condensing firm-wide knowledge into messages that will specifically interest and capture your audience.

SWOT Analysis: SWOT is an acronym that stands for the internal factors of strengths and weaknesses, and the external factors of opportunities and treats. The analysis is a tool for auditing an organization and its environment and is an initial stage of planning that helps marketers focus on key issues. (We use SCOT because we never liked the word "weakness" and prefer instead to think of the "challenges" you may need to address).

Tagline: A brief, evocative slogan or phrase that conveys the most important attribute or benefit of your company, product, or service that you wish to convey in about 10 words or less.

Target Market: See vertical market.

Target Market Effectors: In *The Successful Marketing Plan* (McGraw-Hill, 2003), the authors state that target market effectors are awareness, attitude, trial, and retrial. In other words: Is your market aware of you, do they like you, have they contracted with you, and have they returned?

Vertical Market: A particular industry in which similar products or services are developed and marketed using similar methods. For example, in the broad arena of the design industry, senior living, education, housing, healthcare, and hospitality are considered separate and distinct vertical markets.

Vertical Market Leaders: Selected designers who know a specific market and have the expertise to perform at a high level within the market. They network with the players and prospects in the market and are recognized both internally and externally as experts in that market. Usually principals or associates in the firm.

NOTES

NOTES

NOTES

NOTES

NOTES

NOTES

NOTES

NOTES

NOTES

NOTES